MY FAVORITE FIGHTS

MY FAVORITE FIGHTS

JERRY FITCH

Copyright © 2018 by Jerry Fitch

All rights reserved.

Published by REaD CORNER

ISBN 978-0-473-45944-4

No part of this book/ebook may be reproduced in any form, nor otherwise circulated in any form of cover or binding other than that in which it was published, without written permission from the author; except for the use of brief quotations in a book review.

While the author has made every reasonable effort to determine copyright owners for any/all photographs/images used in this book, there may be some omissions of credits; for which we apologize. Any additions, amendments or corrections can be forwarded to the publisher.

Cover design by Harry Otty © 2018

CONTENTS

Foreword   vii
Introduction   ix

1. Aaron Pryor-Dujuan Johnson — 1
2. Billy Wagner-John Griffin II — 7
3. Bob Foster-Mike Quarry — 15
4. Bobby Chacon-Cornelius Boza-Edwards II — 21
5. Carlos Palomino-Armando Muniz I — 29
6. Carmen Basilio-Johnny Saxton III — 35
7. Cassius Clay-Doug Jones — 39
8. Danny "Little Red" Lopez-Bobby Chacon — 45
9. Doyle Baird-Mike Pusateri I — 51
10. Floyd Patterson-Ingemar Johansson II — 57
11. Freddie Mills-Joey Maxim — 63
12. Freddie Mills-Lloyd Marshall — 69
13. Gene Tunney-Jack Dempsey II — 73
14. Jersey Joe Walcott-Rocky Marciano I — 79
15. Joe Louis-Billy Conn I — 87
16. Joe Louis-Jersey Joe Walcott I — 93
17. Joe Louis-Max Schmeling II — 99
18. Joey Giardello-Rocky Rivero — 105
19. Ken Norton-Larry Holmes — 111
20. Michael Dokes-Gerrie Coetzee — 115
21. Muhammad Ali-Chuck Wepner — 123
22. Palm Springs, California — 127
23. Sugar Ray Leonard-Roberto Duran I — 131
24. Sugar Ray Robinson-Carmen Basilio I — 135
25. Muhammad Ali-Joe Frazier I — 143

Acknowledgments 149
About the Author 151
Also by Jerry Fitch 152

FOREWORD

I grew up in the great sports town of Cleveland, Ohio. We have the Indians, the Browns and the Cavs. At one time though Cleveland was also a great boxing city and it has a rich history in that sport. During the 1960s and beyond Jerry Fitch was a fixture in that history. He knew all of the boxers, managers, trainers, promoters and matchmakers. And all the movers and shakers who passed through. He worked behind the scenes and also covered the fights. His articles have been published in many magazines and newspapers.

Jerry has also traveled the country and the world following his favorite sport. Jerry's passion for boxing and the individuals involved is evident in his four previous books. I have had the pleasure of reading all of Jerry's books and have learned so much about Cleveland's place in boxing lore. This latest effort is surely going to be another hit. I know it was for me.

Foreword

I am proud and honored to call Jerry Fitch my friend and mentor.

Jim Amato

Member of the Boxing Writers Association of America

INTRODUCTION

I started watching boxing in the 1950s as a young boy. In those early days I occasionally watched my parent's small black and white television and the grainy images that appeared on it. I wondered what boxing was all about. That was the start of it all although I didn't realize that fact for several more years. I look back now and recall that those brief glimpses of boxing whet my appetite to eventually see more and learn more. Those Friday night fights and Wednesday night fights from Madison Square Garden and St. Nick's Arena, sponsored by Gillette and Pabst Blue Ribbon Beer, were the catalyst for things to come.

My thoughts and feelings on the countless fights I have witnessed for more than sixty years have made me realize I have been truly blessed to have seen so many wonderful fights and witness so many special fighters. Some of these fights I was fortunate to witness ringside, often from the press

Introduction

row. Many I saw on live television and eventually on closed circuit and other such formats. And last but certainly not least I have viewed hundreds of fights on 8mm and 16mm film and more recently on video and DVD.

As always I must mention that I do not follow boxing anymore. There are many reasons for this and truthfully I don't feel an obligation to explain my reasons. Fortunately I was following boxing during the years where there were many good, even great fighters and countless wonderful fights. Add to that the films and videos I have been able to see over the years of fights that took place long before I was born and I have seen a lot.

While some of the fights I write about may be all time favorites on other lists, I have not selected any particular fight strictly for that reason. My favorites are just that....my favorites. Some of the fights I have selected are probably not the favorites of anyone else but me. Many of the fights I have selected involved fighters I would eventually get to meet. Some even became very good friends. There are many other fights I surely could have included in this book. Some would be obvious choices like the George Foreman- Ron Lyle war of 1976, Sugar Ray Robinson-Jake LaMotta VI in 1951, Marvin Hagler-Thomas Hearns in 1983 etc. I had to draw the line somewhere so I narrowed it down to the ones I have written about on these pages. These fights and fighters that I have chosen are special to me. I can't even explain all of the reasons why they mean so much to me ....they just do.

I have elected to list the chapters randomly and not in any

chronological order. I have simply tried to pick out a varied selection of fights from my extensive list of favorites starting in the 1920s and ending in the 1980s. Enjoy.

August 2018

Aaron Pryor (Author's collection).

1

AARON PRYOR-DUJUAN JOHNSON
NOVEMBER 14, 1981 (CLEVELAND, OHIO)

In my opinion Don King did not put on a lot of fights in his hometown of Cleveland, Ohio. At least not compared to how many he promoted in other cities and countries during his career. On rare occasions he managed to schedule a fight card in Cleveland and I always attended. One such card in November of 1981 featured Cincinnati's Aaron Pryor. Pryor had an outstanding amateur career with a record of 204-16 and won many amateur titles including the National Golden Gloves and National AAU Championships. In 1976 he defeated Thomas Hearns to win the National AAU at 132 lbs. That same year he lost to Howard Davis Jr. at the Olympic box off, serving as an alternate for the 1976 Olympics. By the time the Pryor-Johnson fight was scheduled Pryor had won the WBA Junior Welterweight Championship over Antonio Cervantes and would be defending it for the third time.

Aaron Pryor was a very unorthodox fighter who brought a

lot of excitement to his fights. The "Hawk" as he was called would throw punches from all angles. Heading into this fight he was 28-0 with 26 knockouts. Pryor was 26 years old and his opponent Johnson was a mere 20 years old. Johnson was also undefeated with 17 fights and 13 knockout victories.

Cleveland's Public Auditorium was the venue for the fight. Sometimes it is called Public Hall. It had held many fights over the years that went back to the 1920s when Cleveland's Johnny Risko fought there, both as an amateur and a professional. Today Public Hall is host to many events including induction ceremonies for the Rock and Roll Hall of Fame.

As the fighters were being introduced Pryor danced around the ring and tried to intimidate his younger opponent. Johnson was from the Kronk Gym in Detroit and had Emanuel Steward in his corner. Pryor had the infamous Panama Lewis in his corner. Johnson had advantages in height and reach but he lacked the experience of Pryor.

The announcing team consisted of Tim Ryan, Gil Clancy and Sugar Ray Leonard. They commented on how it appeared Johnson had not warmed up enough, that he was not sweating. But it was Johnson who got off quickly and as Pryor danced around the ring, Johnson floored Pryor with a right hand. He was up without a count. He seemed to laugh off the knockdown. Johnson then staggered Pryor with a left hook and Aaron seemed badly hurt. However Pryor recovered and was coming back into the fight as the round ended.

Johnson continued to throw big punches as the rounds went on. No doubt he was the aggressor. It was only a question as to whether he would be able to land the big punch or run out of gas. Most of his punches were long ones, thrown with the intentions of ending the fight. Pryor was throwing shorter punches and occasionally he seemed to hurt Johnson. What I noticed then and even more after viewing the footage of the fight and Gil Clancy mentioned it more than once, that Johnson had really good head movement and was causing Pryor to miss a lot of his punches.

The early rounds I had to give Johnson the edge because he was landing the bigger shots, he was more effective and as mentioned he managed to bob and weave and cause Pryor's punches to miss. In the fourth round Johnson landed a big right hand that wobbled Pryor. He threw several more bombs and seemed to be in control as the round ended.

As the fifth round started Pryor seemed to step up the pace. I don't know if he intentionally was biding his time or if it just took him that long to figure out Johnson. It might also have been because Johnson had expended so much energy throwing the kind of punches he was launching. He certainly was not pacing himself that's for sure.

In round six they went toe-to-toe again but Pryor landed some solid body shots and his shorter punches were getting through. It seemed the tide was turning and Pryor was taking charge. Johnson was always dangerous but his lack of experience was catching up to him.

Round seven turned out to be the last round of this contest. Just as Gil Clancy was commenting on how Pryor threw punches in bunches and Johnson mainly threw one punch at a time, Pryor landed a big right hand that had

Johnson in trouble. He had him on the ropes and although Johnson was able to make him miss some of his shots, others were landing. As Pryor threw constant punches at Johnson as he was backed into the ropes, referee Jackie Keough stepped in and stopped the fight at 1:49 of the round. Johnson apparently thought he was being given an eight count and held his gloves up high to show the ref he was okay. The crowd booed and Johnson's corner was not happy.

One could argue that the fight shouldn't have been stopped, but it was just a matter of time before Aaron Pryor would have finished him off. He was like a buzzsaw once he hurt Johnson. Clancy remarked that Aaron must have thrown thirty punches in a row before the fight was halted. To referee Keough's credit, Johnson's hands were down at the time of the stoppage and he didn't appear to be able to defend himself. It was only when Keough waved the fight off that Johnson raised his gloves to show him he was okay.

In those days seeing special fighters like Aaron Pryor fight live was something that didn't happen that often in Cleveland. I appreciated being able to witness this fight.

Action from the Pryor vs Johnson fight (Photo-Terry Gallagher)

Billy Wagner attacks John Griffin's body in their second fight. (Photo-Dick Gluszek)

2

BILLY WAGNER-JOHN GRIFFIN II

FEBRUARY 8, 1972 (CLEVELAND)

During the late 1960s, early 1970s Don Elbaum, a native of Erie, Pennsylvania started promoting in the Cleveland/Akron, Ohio area. This enabled several local fighters to finally get some regular fight action and expand their careers. Among the locals were three light-heavyweights: Ray Anderson, John Griffin and Billy Wagner.

Billy Wagner like a lot of local fighters who eventually turned pro was a product of the Golden Gloves tournaments. This Collinwood product won in the Gloves and turned professional in 1968 under the guidance of his older brother Larry Wagner, a former professional fighter himself.

John Griffin was a product of the inner-city of Cleveland and was a star amateur. He won The National A.A.U. Championship in 1966 & 1967 at 175 lbs. When he first turned pro he was under the management of the great Jim Brown, the former Cleveland Brown's running back. John Griffin won his first match on September 25, 1967, at Cobo Arena in Detroit by decision over AJ Staples. He would win eleven of his first twelve fights before losing to Aaron Eastling by points at the Akron Armory.

By the time Billy Wagner would eventually meet up with John Griffin, both men had a lot of experience. Wagner had twenty-eight fights and Griffin had twenty fights. Billy Wagner's best wins had been over former title contender Roger Rouse and Karl Zurheide. John Griffin held two unanimous decision wins over local rival Ray Anderson.

Billy Wagner, sometimes known as Billy Kelly Wagner or Irish Billy Wagner, was signed to meet John Griffin on March 31, 1971 at the Cleveland Arena. In the early going Griffin boxed rings around Wagner. It was one-sided and it appeared that Wagner would be run out of the ring. However Billy had other ideas and launched a comeback that proved to be too little too late. The final tally had Griffin winning a close but unanimous decision.

Larry Wagner, Billy's brother and manager, had tried to get the first fight scheduled for twelve rounds instead of the usual ten. After Billy lost the decision Larry's thinking was that if the fight had gone two more rounds Billy would have won, the way he was coming on at the end.

Soon both parties were trying to come to an agreement for a rematch. Griffin's camp claimed Wagner wanted too big of a purse so the negotiations stalled. In June of 1971 Don Elbaum was trying to match up Big Buster Mathis with Giant Jack O' Halloran at the Cleveland Arena. Later he found out that Mathis had pulled out of a fight in Michigan and was under suspension so he couldn't use him. So he looked for a suitable opponent to meet O' Halloran. Although he barely weighed above the light heavyweight limit, John Griffin stepped forward, much to the shock of everyone concerned. The 6'-6" Jack O' Halloran had a lot of height and a sixty-five pound weight advantage over the light-heavyweight. John Griffin proved everyone wrong as he boxed brilliantly and won a lopsided decision over O'Halloran by scores of 50-41, 49-43 and 49-43. Griffin won all of the rounds less one and made quite the impression on the very small crowd that turned out to witness what they thought was going to be a slaughter.

John Griffin had a reputation of not being afraid to fight anyone and would travel to foreign countries to meet his opponents. After the O' Halloran fight he met WBA Light-heavy Champ, Vicente Rondon in July in Velencia, Spain. He lost the non-title fight but conducted himself admirably while losing the close decision.

As he continued to wait for a return match with Wagner, Griffin seemed to be on a downward slide. He was stopped on a TKO to Jose Luis Garcia in his next bout in October in Caracas, Venezuela. Fighting heavyweights was not the best thing for him but he met them anyway. Griffin and Wagner were finally signed to fight a rematch on December 15, 1971, at the Cleveland Arena. At the last minute Wagner pulled out claiming he had the flu. Because of this he was briefly suspended by the Cleveland Boxing Commission.

Once again Griffin found himself meeting another heavyweight as Buffalo's Vic Brown was brought in as a last minute substitute. I saw John Griffin in his hotel room before this contest and he was a bit under the weather. The way the fight went for the first six rounds you would have never known Griffin wasn't feeling well. He pitched a shutout against the southpaw. But suddenly in the seventh round Brown landed a booming right hand and down went Griffin. He arose but was in bad shape and the fight was stopped to protect him from further punishment.

Even though John Griffin was on a three-fight losing streak he wanted to give Billy Wagner a rematch. After Wagner recovered from the flu and his suspension was lifted, they were signed to meet on February 8, 1972. Larry Wagner wanted a 12-rounder the first time these two met and got his wish for the rematch.

This second fight between the two is one of my favorite fights because I knew both men and felt they would bring a lot to the rematch. My first feature story in Boxing Illustrated in 1971 was titled "Meet John Griffin, The Unknown Title Threat". I met Billy Wagner at the Plain Dealer also in 1971 and eventually did a feature story on his wife, Sandy called "The Fighter's Wife" in 1973, also in Boxing Illustrated. I liked Billy a lot and tried not to let it influence my feelings on the upcoming fight. But no doubt I was pulling for him in the rematch.

The second fight was a lot different than the first. Billy Wagner obviously had a game plan and that was to crowd Griffin and not give him a chance to box at long range like he had the first encounter. Wagner worked Griffin's body with hard punches, especially his left hook. He fought hard and determined and from my view won most all of the rounds with his relentless body attack. It looked from my seat ringside that after the first ten rounds Wagner had a big lead. Griffin started to fight back in the eleventh but it was Wagner's fight to win as long as he finished on his feet.

There is an old rule in boxing that tells a fighter to defend himself at all times. As the bell was just about to ring to end the eleventh round, Wagner dropped his hands and was hit with a hard right hand that caused his legs to dip. Obviously you could debate whether or not the punch landed at the bell or after the bell. What couldn't be debated is that Billy Wagner dropped his hands a moment too soon.

I have never seen any footage of this fight but I was told a few years after the fight by Billy Wagner that he was able to view a home movie someone had taken of the fight. According to Billy at the time he noticed that when the bell rang to start round twelve and he got off his stool to come forward, his legs gave out a bit, he sort of dipped. Apparently he had not recovered in the rest period.

Round twelve, the round that Larry Wagner felt would be the undoing of John Griffin, proved to be the exact opposite. The fighters came out and both were spent but at about the two minute mark of the round Griffin landed a left hook on Wagner. Billy sagged into the ropes and went down. He managed to pull himself up at the count of eight but referee John Christopher took one look at Billy and waved the fight off. It was 2:01 of the final round.

I went into the locker room after the fight and both fighters were pretty banged up. John Griffin's left eye was almost closed and Billy had to have several stitches under his left eye. Billy was beside himself and had to be consoled. He wondered why the fight had to be stopped, felt he had let everyone down. I felt so bad for him because he fought a hell of a fight and was so close to winning. How ironic it was that the two extra rounds Larry Wagner campaigned for proved to be is downfall. The score cards showed that except for referee Christopher, Billy was ahead by plenty going into the last round. He couldn't have lost a decision.

Don Elbaum claimed that John Griffin was going to land a title fight with WBA Light-heavyweight Champ Vicente Rondon after the Wagner win. That was not to be as Rondon instead fought Bob Foster in April for the unified title and got stopped in the second round.

Billy Wagner would go on to win six straight fights and land a very important fight with Mike Quarry at Madison Square Garden on July 21, 1973....but that is a story for another time.

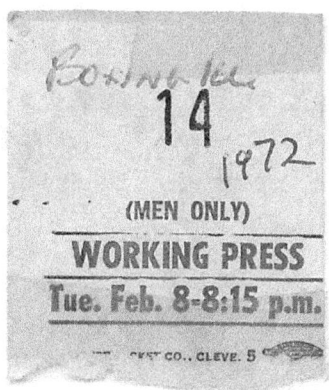

My press pass for the second Billy Wagner vs John Griffin fight in Cleveland (author's collection).

The Author with Bob Foster (Photo-Tony Liccione).

3

BOB FOSTER-MIKE QUARRY

JUNE 27, 1972 (LAS VEGAS)

Bob Foster of Albuquerque, New Mexico was a tall, rangy light-heavyweight with devastating power. At 6' 3 ½ inches tall, he towered over most of his opponents. Like a lot of light-heavyweights, he often felt the need to move up a weight class to gain the big money fights and prestige that came with that division. As many of his fellow light-heavies he did not have a lot of success in the heavyweights. During his career the losses to heavyweights included Doug Jones, Ernie Terrell, Zora Folley, Joe Frazier and Muhammad Ali.

However, when Bob Foster stayed in his weight class he was an amazing fighter. Eventually he got his title shot and on March 24, 1968 in New York, won the light-heavyweight title with a crushing fourth round knockout over champion Dick Tiger. No easy feat as Dick Tiger was a rugged individual who in his entire career of 81 bouts, was only stopped once before and that was by a technical knockout early in his career in Nigeria.

Bob Foster pretty much owned the light-heavyweight division for the next three plus years. Except for an unsuccessful shot at the heavyweight title against Joe Frazier, suffering a knockout in two rounds, on November 18, 1970, he was golden. He successfully defended his title nine times by the time he was signed to give the 21 year- old Mike Quarry a shot at the title.

Mike Quarry, the younger brother of heavyweight Jerry Quarry was a completely different kind of fighter than his brother. Although undefeated at the time he met up with Bob Foster, he was not the big punching brawler his older brother was. He boxed very well but lacked the knockout punch to win big victories inside the scheduled distance. Leading up to the Foster fight, although undefeated in 35 fights he only had a handful of knockout victories and many of those were of the technical variety, or knockouts against opponent type fighters early in his career. When he met the more experienced fighters he found his punch was lacking.

Mike Quarry's record leading into the Foster fight is not sprinkled with a lot of big name victories. Perhaps his biggest wins were over Andy Kendall, Jimmy Dupree and Tommy Hicks. Meanwhile Foster was defending his title for the 10th time, a light-heavyweight record. In addition to stopping WBA Champ Vicente Rondon in two rounds in his previous title defense, he had also defeated Andy Kendall and Tommy Hicks, two opponents Mike Quarry had also met. The difference, however, was that Mike Quarry had to work hard to garnish decisions over both men while Foster knocked them out in title defenses.

I have listed this bout as one of my favorites not because it was some fantastic fight rather because it reminded me of how good Foster was. Mike Quarry should not have been in the ring with someone like Bob Foster, certainly not at that stage of his career.

The "Sheriff" as Foster was called because of his occupation in Arizona, was built on the skinny side for his height. But as they say looks can be deceiving. All of his previous title defense opponents did not last the distance except for Ray Anderson who went the fifteen round distance. It was obvious that Anderson was only in there to survive the fifteen rounds, not to actually win the championship. Everyone else in his nine title defenses failed to make it past the 10th round and most failed to make it make it through the fourth round. Foster defended against Frank DePaula, Andy Kendall, Roger Rouse, Mark Tessman, Hal Carroll, Ray Anderson, Tommy Hicks, Brian Kelly and Vicente Rondon.

Mike Quarry always said it was difficult being the brother of Jerry Quarry. I don't know for a fact but I imagine being Jerry's brother also had benefits. Mike very well may have garnished the title shot against Foster because he was a Quarry. The Quarry name certainly put him in the limelight as his big brother was one of the best known and most popular fighters of his era.

Heading into the fight Bob Foster had a record of 48-5 with 41 knockouts. All of his losses except one were to heavyweights. The light-heavyweight to defeat him was Mauro

Mina and that was is Lima, Peru. Quarry although undefeated in 35 fights looked out of his league to me. I remember leading up to the fight I really wondered how long Mike Quarry would last.

Mike started out real confident and boxed from a distance and at times appeared to be giving an impression of Muhammad Ali as he danced around the ring. He was for the most part boxing a smart fight. Occasionally he would throw a right hand counter but it really didn't seem to have any effect on Foster. By the fourth round Quarry appeared winded and he had his mouth open. Early in the round Foster landed a good left hand on Quarry and Mike apparently decided to trade with the champion. A right hand hurt Quarry, a jab snapped his head back and Foster threw more left jabs. They continued to exchange punches as the bell was about to ring. As Mike Quarry attempted to throw a right hand, Bob Foster landed a devastating left hook that knocked Quarry out cold. There was no saving after the bell so he was counted out by referee Harry Krause. The official time was 3:00 of the fourth round.

It was obvious Mike Quarry was seriously hurt as his corner raced into the ring to attend to him. I think most people watching the fight, especially those at ringside, knew this was no ordinary knockout. Bob Foster was deeply concerned and immediately came over to see how Mike was doing. With the ring doctor and corner working hard to bring Mike around there were some anxious moments. Finally he came to and was helped to the corner.

At the time of the stoppage judge Art Lurie had the fight

14-13 for Foster, and the other two judges Ralph Mosa and Bill Kipp had it 15-12 for Foster. I did not see Quarry winning a single round. The knockout was one of the most brutal I have ever seen. Quarry was lucky he survived that blow and truthfully I am not sure he ever really recovered from it.

Bobby Chacon lands hard right on Boza-Edwards in their 1983 title fight. (author's collection).

4

BOBBY CHACON-CORNELIUS BOZA-EDWARDS II

MAY 15, 1983 (LAS VEGAS, NEVADA)

I could have chosen a couple of Bobby Chacon's fights as my favorites. Chacon was a guy who came to fight every time he entered the ring and more than a few times ended up in a slugging match. He had several thrilling come-from-behind fights in his career including wars with Rafael "Bazooka" Limon in 1982 and Cornelius Boza-Edwards in 1983.

Bobby Chacon started fighting in 1972, mostly in the Los Angeles area. He fought during a time where there were many excellent fighters competing in the area, especially in the lighter weights from 118-135 lbs. As a natural featherweight Bobby would lock horns with many of the best including Arturo Pineda, Frankie Crawford, Chucho Castillo, Ruben Olivares and Danny Lopez.

By 1974 Bobby had a sparkling record of 24-1 with 22 knockouts. His only loss was on June 23, 1973, when he was stopped by a technical knockout in the 9th round against

Ruben Olivares, trying to win the vacant NABF Featherweight title. But after stopping Danny "Little Red" Lopez by a 9th round TKO on March 24th in Los Angeles, he landed a world title shot against Alfredo Marcano for the the WBC Featherweight title. Their match was held on September 7, 1974, in Los Angeles and the fight was stopped in Bobby's favor in the 9th round for a technical knockout victory. "School Boy" Bobby Chacon was champion!

He defended the title once, knocking out Jesus Estrada in the second round on March 1, 1975, but then promptly lost the title in his next fight when Ruben Olivares overwhelmed him in the second round on June 20th, in Inglewood, California.

Through the rest of the 1970s Bobby Chacon continued to battle it out with anyone they threw in front of him. He did defeat Ruben Olivares once and won a piece of a title with a technical decision win over Rafael Limon in seven rounds on April 9, 1979, in LA. That was for the NABF Super Featherweight Title. He then tried for the world title on November 16, 1979, but Alexis Arguello was too much for him and he was stopped by TKO in seven rounds, in Inglewood.

Bobby had a few more fights and worked his way back into another title fight, this time with Cornelius Boza-Edwards for the WBC Super Featherweight Title. Edwards had won the title from Bazooka Limon who had won the title after Alexis Arguello vacated the title to move up to the lightweight division. Chacon met Edwards on May 30, 1981, in Las Vegas, however was stopped by a TKO in the thirteen round.

Never say quit Bobby Chacon went back to the wars in 1982 and ran off five straight wins to land yet another title fight. This time he was to meet one of his old rivals Rafael "Bazooka" Limon, who had defeated Rolando Navarrete for the crown. Navarrete had won the title by defeating Boza-Edwards. Seemed that this Super Featherweight title was constantly changing hands. It was hard to keep track of who was champion if you didn't pay close attention.

Bobby had been fighting in Sacramento for the entire year of 1982 and the title fight was set for there on December 11th. Coming from behind once again and flooring Limon in the 15th round, Bobby Chacon, battered but victorious, won another boxing championship with a 15-round decision. He was now WBC Super Featherweight Champion. As I said, I could include the Limon fight as one of my favorites also because it was a thriller. Although I did not see it live, I have viewed it many times over the years.

This leads me to Chacon's first defense of his newly won crown. Who else should he meet but Cornelius Boza-Edwards! They met on May 15, 1983, in Las Vegas. This one would prove once again to be nothing but pure excitement. You could never count Bobby Chacon out of any fight if he was still standing and still breathing. The Boza-Edwards fight was no different.

This fight started out with Chacon staying on the ropes a lot. Edwards threw a lot of punches from his southpaw stance. He slipped down after a body shot and Richard Steele called it a knockdown. In the second round Chacon floored Edwards with a legit straight right hand, for an eight count. However Chacon suffered a cut over his right eye in this round.

The third round found Bobby Chacon on the deck from a straight left near the end of the round. The "Fight Doctor" Ferdie Pacheco continued to comment on how many punches Chacon was taking and wondered why Bobby seemed to not want to get off the ropes. Always one for the drama, Pacheco seemed to be watching a different fight than I was at times. The action continued after the bell and both fighters had to be lead back to their corners.

As the rounds continued both fighters took turns landing big punches. Chacon was not only bleeding from his cut over the eye but also out of the nose during the fifth round. He had surgery on his nose previously and it seemed to be giving him some trouble breathing. The sixth saw him cut over his left eye also.

During the fight Boza-Edwards got warned several times by referee Richard Steele to stop pushing and using his elbows. Watching Edwards you could see he was using every trick in the book to try to regain the title. He was a skilled technician who conducted himself well in the ring and was no easy mark for anyone.

From the seventh round on the ring doctor kept getting called into the ring to check on Chacon. Ferdie Pacheco felt the fight should have been stopped. He said he feared for Bobby's well-being. You could hear Chacon's corner telling referee Steele that Bobby was okay. At least twice the doctor, then referee Steele were heard saying, "one more round Bobby and I am going to have to stop it." In the eighth round Steele called time to check on Bobby again.

Somehow, some way Bobby continued to rally. By the

eleventh and the start of the twelfth round the doctor didn't even bother to come into the ring to check him again.

The twelfth and final round saw both men exhausted. For several rounds it seemed Bobby couldn't hold up his arms and had them by his side as he launched right hand after right hand. Boza-Edwards no longer had any zip on his punches and his legs were failing him. In close he was throwing pitty-pat punches that wouldn't have hurt anyone. With just over two minutes left in the final round Chacon threw a left and right that floored Edwards again. He got up in bad shape. However either Bobby didn't realize how hurt he was or just had nothing left as he danced around and seemed to be staying away from Edwards and acted like he had the fight won.

At the final bell bruised and battered Bobby Chacon and Cornelius Boza-Edwards embraced. When the final tallies came Bobby Chacon had won a unanimous decision to retain his title. As always Bobby showed courage and determination. You could never count him out. It was the fight of the year.

I rarely agreed with anything Ferdie Pacheco said. But I had to agree with him when he suggested more than once that Bobby should retire. As a matter of fact I had been in touch with Bobby a few times, having met him during one of many trips to LA. I too had hoped he would retire and suggested it to him in a letter. The picture of the postcard in this chapter (page 26) shows his response to me. He fought on for several more years, and although he won all of his fights except his attempt to win the WBA Lightweight title from Ray

"Boom Boom" Mancini, in January of 1984, surely he took punishment that he really shouldn't have taken.

Anyone who still follows boxing closely knows how Bobby spent the last several years of his life. He was loved and embraced by the boxing community and friends without a doubt. But how he ended up is one of the many reasons I have been conflicted about boxing over the years. Somehow boxers need to be protected from themselves because unlike baseball, basketball and a few other sports, where the worst thing that happens if you hang around too long is that you'll embarrass yourself, boxing can leave a fighter with a sad, lasting result.

> Hi Jerry
>
> thanks for your letter. I think it's still in the cards for me to fight. I still have the itch for it. Plus if I do it right I can still make some good money toward my Retirement & family. 1 more round two or three fights at the most.?... If your ever in Oroville look me up. Bobby Chacon

Postcard from Bobby Chacon sent in response to my personal letter to him (author's collection).

The Author with Carlos Palomino (author's collection).

5

CARLOS PALOMINO-ARMANDO MUNIZ I

JANUARY 22, 1977 (LOS ANGELES, CALIFORNIA)

My trips to southern California during the period of 1975-1985, for the most part were never planned in advance. Often when I worked at Republic Steel, later to become LTV Steel, we would have layoffs for various reasons. We did not always get advanced notice as to when we would be off. Many times when I would take a last minute flight to LA, I never knew what to expect. If I got any sort of advanced warning I would call my friend, George Luckman and tell him when I was coming and would also ask him what fights might be taking place during my week or two week visit. Sometimes even though my visits were of a last minute nature I still had a few pleasant surprises. Occasionally special fights were due to take place and because of that I was able to view some amazing fights and fighters. My friend George had a lot of connections and was a regular attendee at many of the major fight cards held in the LA area. He managed to come through with tickets more often than not.

One classic example of a successful unplanned visit was when on January 22, 1977, I was able to attend the Carlos Palomino-Armando "Mando" Muniz welterweight title fight, held at the famous Olympic Auditorium. Palomino had won the title from England's John H Stracey the previous June at Wembley Arena, stopping the champ via a 12th round TKO. He would be making his first defense of the title against fellow Mexican, Muniz. Mando Muniz had two previous title shots against the great Jose Napoles. Many felt his first fight with Napoles was one of the all- time robberies as he cut up Napoles and appeared to stop him. Napoles could not continue after the twelfth round. Somehow Napoles kept his title by a technical decision with the officials claiming that the cuts were caused by head butts from Muniz. The return match was a different story as Mando lost a clear cut 15 round decision to Napoles, in Mexico City. Mexico was Napoles adopted country after he left his native Cuba.

I had been to a few fights at the Olympic Auditorium before. It was an iconic venue with history being made over and over again. The crowds were loud, sometimes crazy. Both Muniz and Palomino were born in Mexico but lived in California for a long time. However it seemed the crowd was more behind Muniz than Palomino. The first round action saw Mando flooring Carlos with a left hook and the crowd went nuts.

In the early going it appeared Mando Muniz was getting

the better of each round. The fight was close however and I felt Muniz was slightly ahead at the half way point. This was in the days of 15 round championship fights. Every so often Mando would land a solid left to Palomino and for whatever reason Carlos couldn't seem to get out of the way of them.

As the fight went along I still had it close. In the later rounds it appeared Carlos Palomino was getting stronger and Mando Muniz was losing a lot of the zip on his punches.

The fight really took a turn in round thirteen when Palomino started teeing off on Muniz and pretty much had his own way with him. In round fourteen the champion really had the upper hand and Muniz was lucky to finish the round on his feet.

Round fifteen is the round they always said made the difference for champions in title fights. Although Muniz was winning early the fight started to become a lot closer around the midway point. Palomino had really put the leather to Muniz in rounds thirteen and fourteen. The final round started the same way and then Palomino landed a series of punches that finally floored Muniz with a little over a minute to go in the round. At around the 2:24 mark of the round referee John Thomas felt the challenger had taken too much punishment and halted the contest.

King Carlos Palomino, as he was sometimes called, was still champion and I was lucky enough to witness it. Later on I found out that both of these game warriors held something else in common. It was a rather unique thing in that they both were college graduates by the end of their ring days.

I was fortunate to meet both of these fine fighters and gentlemen during my days of involvement with The World Boxing Hall of Fame. Mando Muniz was a big part of the group and Carlos Palomino attended some of the yearly award dinners.

Welterweights

Carlos Palomino, *Champion*

1. Pete Ranzany
2. Clyde Gray
3. Pipino Cuevas
4. John H. Stracey
5. Armando Muniz
6. Angel Espada
7. Johnny Gant
8. Randy Shields
9. Miguel Barreto
10. Melvin Dennis

The Ring magazine ratings from March 1977
—post Palomino vs Muniz (Ring Magazine).

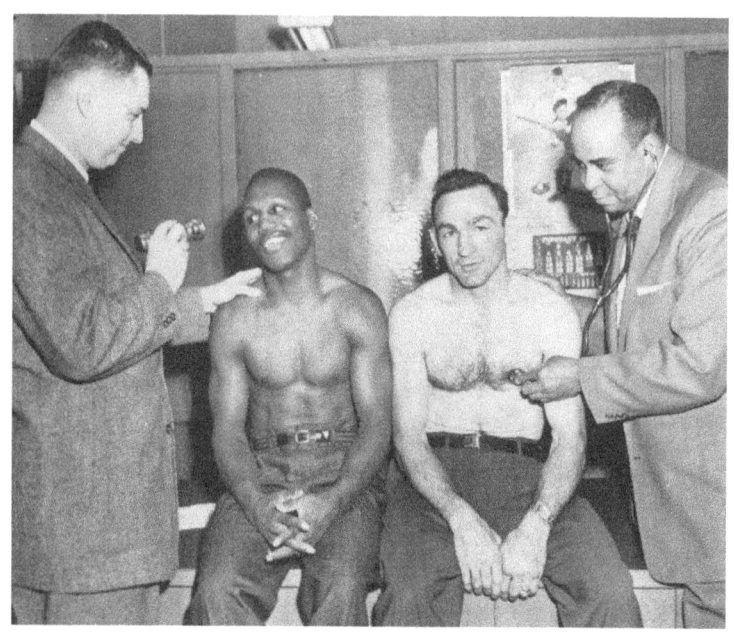

Cleveland Boxing Commission doctors check out challenger Johnny Saxton and champ, Carmen Basilio prior to their third fight (Photo-Plain Dealer).

6

CARMEN BASILIO-JOHNNY SAXTON III

FEBRUARY 22, 1957 (CLEVELAND, OHIO)

The third meeting between World Welterweight Champion Carmen Basilio and former champ Johnny Saxton, certainly will not go down in history as anything special. Unlike their first two fights where Saxton won the title from Basilio and then Carmen regained it in a return bout, this one was anti-climatic. The first two bouts saw Saxton winning a 15-round decision to grab the championship in March of 1956. It was well known that Saxton was a mob-controlled fighter. His title winning fights with Kid Gavilan in 1954 and then his first title fight with Basilio both seemed shady at best. Neither of the fights scoring seemed to coincide with what actually happened during the contest. Basilio came back in September of 1956 with revenge on his mind. This time he left no doubt who the winner was as he battered Saxton and stopped him in the 9th round via a technical knockout to regain the welterweight title. The rubber match of the series had no such drama as it was one-sided and over in the second round. Saxton was floored with a left hook and arose on wobbly legs, forcing referee, Tony LaBranch to stop the contest.

What makes this fight one of my favorites is pretty simple. It was the first live boxing match I ever saw in my life. The fact that I was only ten years old at the time, has really registered with me as I have gotten older. Although I had seen some boxing on television prior to this match and knew a few of the names involved in boxing in the 50s, it didn't really sink in at the time that I was seeing a world championship fight in my very first venture into live boxing. A friend of mine and his father were going to the fights and had an extra ticket and asked me if I could go with them. My parents said I could so off we went to the Cleveland Arena which stood at East 37th and Euclid Avenue.

As I wrote in my *50 Years of Fights, Fighters and Friendships*, I don't even remember any of the under-card, not much really about the whole night except the fact that the main event was over quickly. Twenty odd years later I met Carmen Basilio for the first time and after telling him I had witnessed him in that 1957 fight, he quipped, "Here's your five dollars, you got cheated".

This particular fight would be the only time I ever witnessed Carmen Basilio fight live, but I have been fortunate over the years to watch several of his fights on film and meet former opponents of his like Sugar Ray Robinson, Tony DeMarco, Kid Gavilan and Gene Fullmer. I grew to admire him more and more as I realized that this man from Upstate New York was indeed a real fighter in the truest sense of the word. He gave his all in every fight and was courage personified!

Doug Jones (photo Mike Silver).

7

CASSIUS CLAY-DOUG JONES
MARCH 13, 1963 (NEW YORK CITY)

I was not a Cassius Clay fan in 1963. Although I admire anyone who makes it to the Olympics and wins a gold, I guess Clay's brashness and bold predictions were so far overboard and different from anything I had ever encountered, that he just rubbed me the wrong way. I wanted someone to button his lips so to speak.

When young Cassius Clay (yes, he was still Cassius Clay) signed to fight Doug Jones, a native of New York, I was indeed pulling for Jones. Doug had a pretty good record of 21-3-1 at the time with his only losses coming at the hands of some very good fighters: Eddie Machen, Harold Johnson, and Zora Folley. He was ranked #3 heavyweight in the world, while young Cassius posted a record of 17-0 and was ranked #2.

The fight itself fought in a packed Madison Square Garden attracted all sorts of celebrities. I guess many people besides the regular fight fans wanted to see what all the commotion was about with this guy from Louisville. He had been predicting which round his fights would end. Originally he had picked the sixth round for Jones to fall, but as the fight got closer he lowered it to the fourth round.

As time goes on one's memories sometimes tend to become a little sketchy. So before writing this chapter I decided to view this fight once again to make sure my thoughts and memories hadn't become clouded over the last fifty plus years.

Cassius Clay had a big height, reach and weight advantage over Doug Jones. Jones had actually fought for the light-heavyweight title in 1962, against Harold Johnson, losing a 15-rd decision for the then vacant title. At the weigh-in for the Clay fight he was 188 to Clay's 202 1/2.

The first round saw what perhaps was the best punch of the fight. Ringside announcer, Chris Schenkel was commenting how young Cassius had a bad habit of pulling back, leaning back with his hands down, thus leaving himself open for a countering punch. He had barely gotten those words out of his mouth when Jones landed a big right hand that buckled Clay's knees. Jones tried to follow up but wasn't able to land anymore big blows. As all of us found out over the years Cassius Clay aka Muhammad Ali had a wonderful chin that could take any punch from any of the heavyweights in his era.

As the fight went along there was a lot of give and take. One of the things I didn't remember however, but realized as I watched this fight again in its entirety, was that Cassius missed a lot of punches. I truly didn't remember that he was not as sharp as he would later become. I am not knocking

Doug Jones ability or his effort in this fight. But viewing it I must say I was surprised at how many punches were missed by Cassius Clay.

Although I knew the scoring in this fight I did not allow it to impact my judgment as I scored it myself. I did some work as a judge years ago in both amateur and professional fights, but I don't consider myself a foremost expert. Still at the end of the fight my tally was very similar to the two judges, Artie Aidala and Frank Forbes. My final tally was 5-4-1 for Clay as was theirs. But I also had one or two rounds where I could have scored it the other way, for Jones instead of Clay. What amazed me is how the referee Joe LoScalzo scored it 8-1-1 for the "Louisville Lip". What fight was he watching is beyond me. No way Clay won eight rounds.

I think if there was any reason Jones may not have been given the nod it is because of the last couple of rounds. Although both men seemed tired, Jones seemed to lose his energy more and Cassius Clay threw far more punches and was way more active.

Jones being a native New Yorker really had the crowd behind him. When he threw punches, even if they did not land solidly, the crowd roared. When Clay's prediction of a fourth round knockout did not come true, they actually booed him. Jones gave a terrific effort and I must say I understand how after all these years some longtime fans feel he won the fight and was robbed. He was not robbed! I am sure history might have been different had Doug Jones won this fight. This is not to say that Cassius Clay, later known as Muhammad Ali wouldn't have continued on, won the title and went on to greatness. But a defeat early on may have side-tracked his march to the title, if ever so briefly.

In my opinion boxing needed a savior back in 1963. Although I loved Floyd Patterson, when Sonny Liston destroyed him twice in only one round, the heavyweight division felt different. Sonny was not exactly a warm and friendly guy who had a huge following. Make no mistake about it the Clay-Jones fight did not involve some great conspiracy. It was a close fight that perhaps could have gone either way. After viewing it again and scoring it myself, I see nothing wrong with the decision.

I did not jump on the Clay/Ali bandwagon after this bout. But I was drawn to watching this young fighter more and more. I realized he was different. Yes, he irritated a lot of people with his big mouth. But if you were a true boxing fan you had to admire his ability.

Heavyweights

Sonny Liston, *Champion*

1. Floyd Patterson
2. Cassius Clay
3. Doug Jones
4. Ingemar Johansson
5. Zora Folley
6. Cleveland Williams
7. Robert Cleroux
8. Billy Daniels
9. Archie Moore
10. Henry Cooper

The Ring's heavyweight ratings for February 1963.
(Ring Magazine)

The Author with Danny 'Little Red' Lopez (author's collection).

8

DANNY "LITTLE RED" LOPEZ-BOBBY CHACON

MAY 24, 1974 (LOS ANGELES)

I didn't start traveling to California until 1975 and will always be grateful for the ten plus years I was able to go there. I saw a lot of good fights and even better met many famous boxers and boxing personalities. I also developed some longtime friendships and till this day I still communicate with many Californians on Facebook.

Before I started venturing to the west coast the undefeated Danny "Little Red" Lopez met up with once-beaten Bobby "School Boy" Chacon at the Los Angeles Sports Arena. This fight took place on May 24, 1974. Both of these little gamecocks were making noise in the featherweight division at the time and their fight was to be a real local showdown. Chacon's only loss had been to the great Ruben Olivares. Lopez was looking to continue up the ladder with a win over Bobby Chacon.

At the weigh-in Chacon hit the scales at 123 1/2 while Lopez had a bit of a weight advantage at 126. Lopez was also

45

three inches taller. Chacon had met better opposition overall with wins over Frankie Crawford, Arturo Pineda and Chucho Castillo on his resume. He was installed as a 10-8 favorite.

The fight had barely started when Bobby Chacon began throwing right hand leads and was landing them most of the time. Anyone who followed Lopez' career knows he was not the greatest defensive boxer. Already he had a bruise by his left eye as the round ended.

The second round continued the same way and although Lopez did flurry at times it appeared Chacon was ducking most of the punches and showing pretty good defense. Chacon was also able to land his right hand almost at will. Adding to his woes Danny's right eye began streaming blood from a cut in his eyebrow.

In the third round Chacon actually turned Lopez around with a right hand. Danny eventually did land a good right of his own and then a left hook. But Chacon had a big flurry at the end of the round that just may have pulled it out for him.

In round four Danny Lopez was finally on the attack just as a fire cracker went off in the crowd. He seemed to be finally getting the better of Chacon in some of the exchanges for the first time. Little Red may have won his first round.

Round five was fairly even but I couldn't see anyone scoring it for Lopez as Chacon was the busier fighter. He continued to fight with energy and threw many very good right hands, most of which landed.

Round six was a pivotal round in many ways. Lopez perhaps landed his best punches of the fight and appeared to be coming back into the battle. But at the end of the round, although Chacon's nose started to bleed, Bobby landed two real good left hooks and reopened the cut over Danny's right eye.

Lopez came out in round seven with a bit of desperation and landed a big right hand. They traded rights and then Chacon came back with a combination of his own as the round carried through fairly even.

In round eight Lopez was obviously way behind in the scoring. He tried to box but in every exchange Chacon seemed to be getting the best of it. Bobby often telegraphed his right hand leads yet Danny could not seem to get out of the way of them.

Round nine started quickly and Chacon came tearing out of his corner and immediately landed a huge right hand that staggered Lopez. It was a flurry of punches from that instance, right, right, left, right, and Lopez was driven helplessly into the far corner, and was hung up on the ropes. Although referee John Thomas was watching closely he didn't intervene. Fortunately Lopez was knocked down from mostly glancing blows and not more seriously hurt while in that precarious position. He took the mandatory count but when Chacon resumed his attack it was obvious Lopez had no defense and Referee Thomas stepped in and stopped the fight at 48 seconds of the 9th round.

The Lopez victory launched Bobby Chacon into a title match with Alfredo Marcano where he won the WBC World Featherweight Title with a 9th round TKO. He would lose the title in his first defense via a 2nd round TKO to Ruben Olivares. Of course Chacon would have many other thrilling fights in his career and eventually win the WBC Super-featherweight crown before he retired for good in 1988.

Ruben Olivares would lose his WBC title to David Kotey in September of 1975. I attended that title fight at the then Inglewood Forum. Lopez came back from the Chacon defeat and won the featherweight title two years later over the same David Kotey. He would hold that WBC crown for over three years and eight title defenses before losing it to the great Salvador Sanchez by a 13th round TKO in February of 1980. He lost a return match to Sanchez by a 14th round TKO in June of 1980 and immediately retired.

Featherweights

Title Vacant

1. Eder Jofre
2. Ernesto Marcel
3. Art Hafey
4. Danny Lopez
5. Leonel Hernandez
6. Ruben Olivares
7. Bobby Chacon
8. Jose Legra
9. Santos Luis Rivera
10. Jose Antonio Jiminez

The Ring magazine ratings from March 1974 (Ring Magazine).

Mike Pusateri (left) and Doyle Baird square-up prior to their fight in Cleveland (Photo-Charlie Harris-Plain Dealer)

9

DOYLE BAIRD-MIKE PUSATERI I
FEBRUARY 16, 1971 (CLEVELAND)

During Don Elbaum's time promoting fights in Cleveland and Akron, Ohio, he had some hits and misses. I have written about Don in my book, "50 Years of Fights, Fighters and Friendships". In the chapter about Don Elbaum I made it quite clear that Don sometimes got excited and a bit carried away with his announcements about major fights he claimed to have locked up for Cleveland. Yet many never even came close to fruition. Still I did give Don credit for two major things in his time promoting here. First of all he brought in some really famous fighters that many of us would have never seen if it were not for him. That list included Emile Griffith, Floyd Patterson, Ernie Terrell, Cleveland Williams, George Foreman and Ken Norton. Secondly Don enabled many local fighters to stay busy with their careers and fight often before their hometown fans. That list included such fighters as Billy Wagner, John Griffin, Earl Johnson, Frankie Kolovart, Chuck Spencer,

Bobby Haymon, Art Harris, Terry Daniels and Ted Gullick. And last but certainly not least was Akron's Doyle Baird.

Doyle Baird was an Akron middleweight that Don just happened to manage. Of course promoters are not legally supposed to manage fighters so Don had his father Max, back in Erie, Pa. listed as Doyle's manager. Doyle had served time in Mansfield Reformatory in Ohio and came up the hard way on the streets. But once he started fighting he became focused. Don started him out in 1966 fighting mostly locally in Akron, and other Ohio cities and occasionally in such places as Pittsburgh, Buffalo and Indianapolis.

Throughout 1966 and 1967 Doyle Baird was matched with opponents like Tommy Shaffer, Sam Sellers, Carl Jordan and Stewart Gray. Finally on March 20, 1968 he was matched with a fighter named Ernie Burford. Although his professional record wasn't stellar Burford had been in with most of the best welterweights and middleweights in the world including Joey Giardello, Freddie Little, Luis Rodriquez and George Benton. He held wins over Henry Hank, Sugar Boy Nando and Rubin Carter. Baird defeated him over ten rounds in Akron for perhaps his first major win.

On June 28, 1968 Doyle Baird was matched with another tough fighter. His opponent Ted Wright would go on to win over fifty fights in his career and he too fought many of the really good fighters. Wright had met Emile Griffith, Luis Rodriquez and Nino Benvenuti. His resume showed wins over Phil and Denny Moyer, Federico Thompson and Don Fullmer. Doyle won the 10-rounder in Akron. This launched him into a non-title fight with World Middleweight Champion, Nino Benvenuti at the Akron Rubber Bowl on October 14, 1968. Doyle in my opinion was robbed when the fight was called a draw.

Doyle Baird started a nice win streak after the Benvenuti disappointment and that included a split decision win over Don Fullmer on October 29, 1969 at the Cleveland Arena. Doyle was cut badly over his left eye and had to have more than a dozen stitches to close his wounds.

By the time Doyle Baird was scheduled to fight Mike Pusateri for the first time at the Cleveland Arena on February 16, 1971, he had lost a unanimous decision to Emile Griffith, got stopped in ten rounds in a return with Nino Benvenuti in Bari, Italy and had knocked out one time Cleveland middleweight hopeful Earl "Sugarcane" Johnson in two rounds in Cleveland.

Mike Pusateri had a storied career fighting out of Brockton, Massachusetts. He was a big puncher who started out fighting at light-heavyweight which did not work out well for his short stature. Eventually he realized that middleweight was more to his liking. Most of his career he was trained by Allie Colombo who had been one of Rocky Marciano's trainers during "The Rock's" career. There was no doubt that Mike could punch. Unfortunately Pusateri was very prone to cuts and suffered several losses because of them. Heading into his first fight with Doyle Baird his overall record was 29-15-4. He started out his career winning seventeen straight fights but then began to meet tougher opposition. He lost two tough fights to rival Joe DeNucci by decision, one a majority one. Perhaps his biggest win came against South Africa's Willie Ludick, who he stunned with a surprising knockout in the second round in Capetown, South Africa in January of 1966.

As mentioned "Iron Mike" as he was often called lost many as his fights because he was prone to cuts. When I met Mike in 1971 while working at the Plain Dealer, he told me that when he was younger he never got cut. He felt that all of the years working over the hot ovens and steam tables in the family restaurant weakened his skin. He worked as a chef in that Italian restaurant in Dedham, Mass., a suburb of Boston. It was a real passion for him.

Calling this fight one of my favorites was easy. It was a good match between two bleeders who came to fight. Also there was some humorous moments for me that I have never forgotten. While sitting ringside I sat next to a former business agent for one of the unions at the Cleveland Plain Dealer. This was during the days that people were allowed to smoke in arenas. This man who I casually knew from my time at the Plain Dealer was not exactly enamored with Mike Pusateri. He had no clue who Pusateri was and although Italian himself he was making comments about Mike that were not too kind to say the least. He puffed away on a big old stogie and one of his remarks was "Where on earth did they dig up this ugly SOB?" Then to add fuel to the fire when Mike Pusateri came into the ring, Mike already had his gloves on. However when it came time to take off his robe they couldn't get it over the gloves and had to take scissors and cut the sleeves. It took a while for his corner men to find the scissors and the crowd started laughing. Then for some odd reason they had trouble locating Pusateri's mouthpiece.

When the fight started Mike Pusateri showed he had come to fight. Baird was no stranger to tough battles and Iron Mike was in this fight to give him just that. In the early going I had Pusateri ahead and in the fourth round he got Doyle Baird in some serious trouble. As the fight continued the crowd of just under 4,000 really got into the fight. Two men slugging, bleeding, a real crowd-pleasing kind of fight is just what they were looking for. In round seven Pusateri dropped the game Akronite. Doyle popped back up but was obviously hurt.

Baird won the last three rounds on the scorecards and thought he won the battle. When the announcement was made referee Vito Mazzeo scored it 46-43, judge Jimmy Tryina tallied 47-45 and judge Tony LaBranche called it 45-44, all for Pusateri. Apparently Mike's early work had given him enough of a lead to earn the victory.

Baird suffered a gash over his left eyebrow and Pusateri was bleeding as usual. I think a rematch was on Don Elbaum's mind and in the works before the fighters left the Arena. Finally the guy next to me with the cigar quipped, "I still don't know where they dug up this guy!"

The Author with Floyd Patterson (author's collection).

10

FLOYD PATTERSON-INGEMAR JOHANSSON II

JUNE 20, 1960 (NEW YORK)

Beginning with their first bout in June of 1959 Floyd Patterson and Sweden's Ingemar "Ingo" Johansson had a three fight trilogy that saw some very important heavyweight boxing history being made. For good reasons many critics felt Patterson had not been meeting the top contenders. His manager Cus D'Amato was picking and choosing who he wanted Patterson to defend against. Many felt Cus was just taking the easy way out but there was more to it than that. Amato had waged war on the powers that be, not willing to be a puppet to the Jim Norris controlled International Boxing Club. He refused to match Floyd with any fighter that was controlled by the International Boxing Club. Eventually that organization was broken up as a monopoly by the courts and then investigated by Senator Estes Kiefauver and his committee and a trial was set. Attorney General Robert Kennedy was the prosecutor in the trial. It was proven that the IBC had ties to the mafia. After three months defendants Frankie Carbo, Blinky Palermo and several others were sentenced to prison and the IBC was finished.

When Rocky Marciano retired as undefeated heavyweight champion, Floyd Patterson and Archie Moore were matched for the vacant title. On November 30, 1956 Floyd Patterson won the heavyweight championship with a convincing fifth round knockout. After that he defended the title four times against the likes of Tommy Jackson, Pete Rademacher (In Pete's first professional fight), Roy Harris and Brian London.

Ingemar Johansson was from Gothenburg, Sweden and fought all of his early fights in Europe. His biggest wins were a fifth round kayo over Henry Cooper and then he won the European Heavyweight Title with a thirteenth round knockout over Joe Erskine. What really landed him the world title shot however was when he stunned outstanding contender, Eddie Machen with a brutal knockout in the first round on September 14, 1958, in Gothenburg.

When Patterson and Johansson met the first time on June 26, 1959 most fans surely thought it would be another successful title defense for Patterson. European heavyweights were not held in high esteem. But Ingo landed his famed right hand on Floyd in the third round and after seven knockdowns the fight was mercifully stopped for a TKO win for Johansson. He made history as Sweden's first ever world champion.

Which brings us to the rematch. Throughout history several heavyweight champions had lost their crown and failed in an attempt to win it back. James J. Corbett failed, so did Bob Fitzsimmons, Jack Dempsey, Max Schmeling, Ezzard Charles and Jersey Joe Walcott. All failed in return matches. This total does not include several champions, since Patterson's reign, who failed to regain the title once they lost it in the ring. Those names include Joe Frazier, Larry Holmes.

Back in the days of Floyd Patterson most major fights had return bout clauses in the contracts. So, almost within a week of being a year later, Floyd squared off with Johansson hoping to do something that had never happened before....regaining the heavyweight title. Floyd and Ingo met on June 20, 1960 in The Polo Grounds in New York. The crowd was announced as 31,892.

Floyd came in at 190 lbs. which was 8 lbs. more than their first fight. Trainer Dan Florio felt Floyd was too light the first fight and the additional weight would make Floyd stronger and even add punching power. Johansson was 194 3/4, close to his weight for the first contest. Johansson was installed an 8-5 favorite in the betting.

The referee for this contest was Arthur Mercante, who would be the third man in the ring for his first world championship. History would show that this man was indeed an excellent official. He would go on to referee many major championships during his career.

After Jack Dempsey, Gene Tunney and many other former champions and dignitaries were announced the fighters were brought together for their final instructions. Chris Schenkel was the commentator along with Marty Glickman.

Round one saw the men circling the ring and eventually Floyd landed two good lefts, missed a couple off balance shots and continued to move around. He looked confident. Already there was some swelling under Ingo's left eye. Patterson's round.

In round two again Patterson was the aggressor but Ingemar was boxing better than in the first round. Suddenly Johansson landed a big right hand that shook Floyd although he didn't look to be going down. Patterson was back peddling and regaining his poise but the punch must have brought back bad memories of their first meeting so he was much more careful the rest of the round. The fact Patterson took the punch and wasn't decked must have given him confidence. Johansson's round.

As round three began Patterson came out jabbing and Johansson was pawing with his own left. They traded jabs and then Floyd started going to the body with some of his shots. Patterson had mainly thrown lefts from a distance, but he did land a good right hand. Patterson's round.

In round four Patterson continued to box and seemed to get the better of most of the exchanges. With less than a minute to go Arthur Mercante warned Ingo for holding. It was not the first time. Patterson's round.

Early in the fifth round Patterson landed a good right and then a booming left hook that sent Johansson down on his back. He got up at nine with his mouth bleeding. Patterson went into an all- out flurry of punches, some landing, some not. Johansson stumbled and turned sideways and Floyd yanked him and turned him around to face him. Chris

Schenkel had just commented that there was a minute and a half left in the round when Floyd launched and landed one of the best left hooks you could ever hope to see. Johansson crashed to the canvas and did not move except for his left foot twitching. Mercante counted him out at 1:51 seconds of the fifth round.

The crowd roared and Floyd smiled at the crowd with the look of satisfaction like "I told you so". It was history and redemption for Floyd. Once he saw that Johansson was possibly seriously hurt he tried to get over and help him but was pushed back by Johansson's trainer Whitey Bimstein and others. It took a long time for Ingo to regain his senses and his feet. Howard Cosell was in the ring and was interviewing Patterson, who was his usual modest and polite self. When Cosell tried to get an interview with Johansson Whitey Bimstein said it would not be possible.

The fight resulted in Patterson being named The Fighter of the Year and the fight, Fight of the Year by Ring Magazine. Floyd Patterson's name was forever etched in history as the first two-time heavyweight champ.

These two men would go on to fight once more in 1961 with Floyd again knocking out Johansson, this time in the sixth round. But their second fight will always be a very special moment in boxing.

Al DelMonte, Jack Kearns and Joey Maxim, London 1950 (author's collection).

11

FREDDIE MILLS-JOEY MAXIM

JANUARY 24, 1950 (LONDON, ENGLAND)

Cleveland has had many great fighters in its history. However there have not been many world champions among that group. One of them however was a slick boxing Italian from the Collinwood area of Cleveland. Giuseppe Antonio Berardinelli was born in Cleveland on March 28, 1922.

The story goes when Joey was young and starting out as an amateur boxer one of his longtime friends and later first manager, Vic Rabersak, suggested Joey change his name to Maxim, in honor of the Maxim gun, a type of machine gun invented in 1883. Joey's rapid fire left jab was why the name was chosen. It was often said rather jokingly that there wasn't a boxing robe, marquee, poster or boxing program large enough to fit his entire name. Thus he became Joey Maxim.

Joey Maxim had an excellent amateur career and was a local Golden Gloves Champion. In 1940 he won both the National Golden Gloves and National AAU Championships at 160 lbs. Even at a young age he showed excellent boxing skills and toughness. His left jab was his main weapon and it served him well throughout his career.

Joey Maxim like other fellow Clevelanders who went into the pro ranks in the early 1940s found out there were an awful lot of good boxers around. Unlike today you had to fight often and the competition was fierce to say the least. In 1941, Joey's first year as a pro, he was in with the likes of Lee Oma, Nate Bolden and Red Burman. In 1942 it got even tougher as he met Booker Beckwith, Jimmy Bivins, Curtis Sheppard and Ezzard Charles twice.

In 1943 Joey Maxim suffered his first and only knockout loss as Curtis "Hatchetman" Sheppard caught him cold and stopped him in the first round on March 10th in Cleveland. His head was driven through the ropes and some at ringside feared his neck was broken. This is where Joey Maxim proved his toughness as he was back in the ring three weeks later against the same Curtis Sheppard and won a decision over ten rounds.

Joey wasn't afraid to fight heavyweights either. His manager Doc Kearns matched him up with Johnny Flynn, Buddy Walker, Phil Muscato, even Jersey Joe Walcott three times. By the end of 1949 Joey had a record of 67-16-4. Three of his losses were to the great Ezzard Charles, one to Jimmy Bivins, two to Jersey Joe Walcott and one to Lloyd Marshall. He was meeting all of the best in two divisions.

At the end of 1948 and beginning in 1949 Joey had wins over Bob Satterfield, a return match with Jimmy Bivins, and a fifteen round loss to Ezzard Charles. He then was matched with Gus Lesnevich, former World Light-heavyweight Champion on May 23, 1949 in Cincinnati, Ohio. It was for the vacant American Light-heavyweight Title and he won the decision in fifteen rounds. Three more wins to finish out the year and he finally got what all fighters strive for....a title fight. Doc Kearns signed him to meet England's Freddie Mills in London for the world title.

Freddie Mills was defending his championship for the first time. He had two fights after his title-winning effort against Gus Lesnevich on July 26, 1948. He knocked out Johnny Ralph in the 8th round on November 6, 1948, in Johannesburg. Then attempting to win the British and Empire Heavyweight Title he was stopped in the 14th round by champion, Bruce Woodcock, in London on June 2, 1949.

Freddie and Joey met for their title match at Earls Court Empress Hall in London on January 24, 1950. The large crowd included many celebrities including American actors Gene Simmons and Gregory Peck. Ring Magazine's sage Nat Fleischer was also sitting ringside as he normally was at major fights.

In round one it was apparent what Freddie Mills and his corner had in mind. Most likely they felt there wasn't a chance for Freddie to outbox Maxim in a long fight. Mills came out of his corner fighting hard and launching punches. He landed a wicked left hook that hurt Joey and made his knees buckle. However Joey was not only a good boxer, he had an excellent chin so he recovered quickly. Although Mills continued his attack he couldn't get off anymore hard punches to match his first assault.

Mills had a pretty good second round but you could see by watching the film that Maxim was starting to make a move, he was starting to counter inside. The crowd was all for Mills so when he did throw punches, even when they didn't land cleanly, they roared.

In rounds three and four things started to change for Mills. Maxim cornered him and landed a series of punches both to the head and some hard punches just under Mill's heart. Freddie for the first time was not firing back and only covering up.

The next three rounds were mostly in Joey's favor as he used his left jab and moved around the ring smartly. Joey Maxim had excellent foot work. Critics of Joey Maxim often said he was boring, that he didn't excite many fans because he lacked the big knockout punch. However more than a few experts, who I truly had a lot of respect for including Angelo Dundee, said that if you wanted to show a young fighter how to become a good boxer, it would be wise to show footage of Joey Maxim's fights. His footwork, jab and ability to tie up an opponent were fine examples of how to box correctly.

In round eight Mills attempted to come back into the fight and showed a bit of desperation as he clumsily threw punches hoping to stop Maxim or at the very least counter his attack. He launched his left hook and had Maxim backing up a bit. It was to no avail however and as Mills went back to his corner it was obvious he was a very tired fighter.

Round nine saw both men exchanging but it was obvious Maxim was getting the better of every exchange. After the fight it was revealed that Mill's corner actually removed three of his front teeth between rounds. Needless to say he was hurting and beginning to swallow his own blood.

The film of the Mills-Maxim fight is a beauty. I have always appreciated the fact the late, great Jim Jacobs was kind enough to sell me a copy of the fight. But for all the clarity and professional filming of the event apparently even the cameraman was shocked and caught off guard when in the 10th round Joey whipped over a left and right hand that floored Mills. Those punches are missing from the footage. One moment they are going at it and the next you see Mills on the canvas where he is counted out by the referee, Andrew Smyth.

Joey Maxim was World Champion! Freddie Mills retired after the fight after a long 14 year career with 97 recorded fights. Nobody really knows how many fights he had in the boxing booths prior to his official professional career.

Joey Maxim defended his title twice in 1951 and 1952 against Irish Bob Murphy and then Sugar Ray Robinson. The Robinson fight of course is discussed over and over because of the fact the heat did in Robinson and he couldn't come out for the 14th round. Joey would finally defend his title against Archie Moore, who had waited it seemed forever for a title shot. On December 17, 1952 the "Old Mongoose" won the title over Joey in a 15-round decision in St. Louis.

Joey would challenge Archie Moore two more times for the championship and lose decisions both times in 1953 in Utah and 1954 in Miami. Joey brought himself and the city of Cleveland glory on January 24, 1950, when he won the World Championship.

Lloyd Marshall (right) stuns Freddie Mills in the first round of their 1947 fight in London (Gilbert Odd photo)

12

FREDDIE MILLS-LLOYD MARSHALL

JUNE 3, 1947 (LONDON, ENGLAND)

When I was collecting boxing films during the 1970s and 1980s I was always trying to find films that featured Cleveland fighters. It was not easy and often frustrating because even though historically Cleveland had some really good, even great fighters very little footage exists. You would think with big-time fighters like Johnny Kilbane, Johnny Risko, Jimmy Bivins to name just three, there would be all sorts of footage available. But it is very limited and in some cases non-existent as in the case of Johnny Risko. To this day, even though Risko had approximately 140 pro fights including meeting thirteen world champions, I have never found any film on his career.

Another one of Cleveland's greats was Lloyd Marshall who campaigned as a middleweight and light-heavyweight during some of the best years of boxing. He met twelve champions and defeated nine of them. Yet there are only a few of his fights available for the viewing public.

I was very happy when in late 1979 or early 1980 Jim Jacobs, who owned the largest collection of fight films in the world, offered me a copy of Lloyd Marshall's fight with Freddie Mills which took place in 1947 in London. I was thrilled even more when I first viewed it to find that it was of excellent quality.

By the time Freddie Mills and Marshall met, Lloyd was on the downside of his very productive career. And even though Freddie Mills would ultimately win the World Light-heavyweight title five bouts after his match with Marshall, he too could have been considered well past his prime. Freddie had many tough battles in his career, many not recorded from his boxing booth days.

I once wrote a story on this fight for the British magazine *Boxing Monthly* in May of 1990. I titled it "The Tune Up" because quite frankly I felt that Mill's management probably thought Marshall was finished as a contender and a win over him would look good on Freddie's resume. It would also help him toward his quest of landing a return match with champion Gus Lesnevich. Mills had fought a heroic battle with Lesnevich the first time in May of 1946 before being stopped via a 10th round TKO.

Prior to meeting Mills, Lloyd Marshall had lost two of his previous three bouts, both by knockouts to Ezzard Charles and Oakland Billy Smith. I am sure he looked like easy pickings for Freddie. To say they were dead wrong would be an understatement and thankfully this fight was filmed and saved so many of us could appreciate seeing Lloyd Marshall in action. This was not his prime but one can only imagine what he looked like in his earlier years. He was an amazing fighter.

The fight started and in a matter of moments Lloyd Marshall landed a stunning left hook on Mills and although it did not floor him, it literally paralyzed him. Freddie stumbled near the ropes and turned to face Marshall who was completely on the other side of him. He had no idea where he was and I think even Marshall was caught off guard and hesitated in following up. Otherwise the fight would have been over then and there.

The announcers input obviously came after this fight was completed because he talked in the past tense concerning the fight. He mentioned more than once that Mill's never recovered from that first big punch. He fought back and survived the first round however.

Mills was knocked down to one knee from a left hook in the second round and Marshall was moving around the ring nicely. He seemed to be in charge and not a worry on his mind. Mills could not land any worthy punches.

Round three was a disaster for the British Empire Champ. He took a right to the heart and was down for an eight count from that. Barely up and fighting back Mills absorbed three lighting fast rights and went down for a count of five. Nobody could ever say Mills wasn't trying to stem the tide and he managed to get off one of his own famed left hooks and staggered Marshall. It made me cringe to hear the narrator refer to Lloyd as "The colored boy". Mind you this footage came from 1947, still it made me uncomfortable the first time I viewed this film.

Round four was the only round Mills held his own. Once again he staggered Marshall with a solid left hook. He was also warned for perhaps the fourth or fifth time in the fight for holding. Mills may have actually won this round as he staggered Marshall again, this time with a right hand just as the bell was about to ring.

The fourth round rally must have been the last hurrah for Freddie. The fifth had barely begun when a left hook floored him again and he got up to one knee and was counted out without making much of an effort to rise. It appeared Freddie decided to call it a day then and there.

After the fight I am sure Lloyd Marshall and his team finally felt they would get a title shot with this big win. But in his next fight Marshall was stopped by Ezzard Charles in the second round. The following year Mills was given a return match with Gus Lesnevich and won the World Light-heavyweight title. Lloyd never came close to a title shot ever again. Less than two years after winning the championship Freddie Mills, in his first title defense would lose the crown to Cleveland's Joey Maxim via a tenth round knockout on January 24, 1950. He then retired.

13

GENE TUNNEY-JACK DEMPSEY II

SEPTEMBER 22, 1927 (CHICAGO, ILLINOIS)

There are many fights that have gone down in boxing history as all-time great fights for a lot of reasons. Although more than a few of my favorites are not all-time greats the second Tunney-Dempsey or if you prefer, Dempsey-Tunney fight certainly is one of the all-time great fights on my list.

The second Tunney fight perhaps made a fighter like Jack Dempsey even more famous than he already was. Losing a fight in the fashion Jack did left a lasting impression for many followers. I think it is safe to say when talking about Dempsey's career one of the first fights people mention is the second Tunney fight.

Jack Dempsey had 79 recorded fights in his career and nobody really knows how many un-sanctioned or un-recorded fights he had. But historians, even casual fans always seem to mention certain fighters when discussing who was the best ever in heavyweight annuals. Those names most always include Jack Johnson, Joe Louis, Rocky Marciano and Muhammad Ali. And you can usually add Jack Dempsey's name in that conversation too.

Jack Dempsey's career was without a doubt one of the most historic ever. His story of fighting in small towns, mining camps, riding the rails and basically coming up the hard way is one of the greatest stories ever. He seemed to be almost larger than life at times. His matches with Jess Willard, Luis Angel Firpo, Tommy Gibbons, Jack Sharkey and eventually Gene Tunney also had elements of controversy. His title winning fight against Jess Willard in Toledo, Ohio on July 4, 1919 was one of the biggest beat downs ever witnessed. Dempsey was like a wildcat and literally beat Willard to a pulp to win the world championship. Later there was stories that Dempsey's gloves were loaded. This was never proven but the story lingers to this day.

The Tommy Gibbons fight in Shelby, Montana on July 4, 1923 will forever be famous but not for the fifteen rounds of boxing between the two men. The promotion was such a disaster that the town of Shelby actually went broke.

The Luis Firpo fight on September 14, 1923 in New York is another of Dempsey's fights that has lasted in conversation throughout history. Not because Dempsey retained his title with a second round knockout rather because Dempsey was knocked through the ropes in the first round by the "Wild Bull of the Pampas". Ringside reporters were shown helping Dempsey as he fell and then pushing him back into the ring. The referee had counted to four before Dempsey got back into the ring. The fight was all Dempsey's. He had floored

Firpo seven times in the first round and twice more in the second before stopping him for good. The controversy about Dempsey being helped back into the ring has lasted forever. Even famous artist George Bellows made sure the scene would be etched in history with one of his famous paintings showing Dempsey being knocked through the ropes.

Jack Dempsey defended his title for the sixth time on September 23, 1926 against Gene Tunney in Philadelphia. The fight although a title defense was set for ten rounds. Tunney won the title in a one-sided fight that saw Gene box Jack's ears off. It looked like Dempsey's days as a fighter were coming to a close.

On July 21, 1927 Jack Dempsey met former heavyweight champion, Jack Sharkey in a 10-round match. Both men were seeking one last title shot. Once again Jack Dempsey won but not without controversy. In the seventh round it appeared Dempsey hit Sharkey low and when Sharkey turned to complain to the referee Dempsey hit him with a left hook and ended the fight. This launched him into a rematch with Gene Tunney. The fight was set for September 22, 1927 at Soldier's Field in Chicago. The crowd was over 100,000 and the gate was $2,658,660. It was the first $2 million gate in entertainment history.

The fight introduced new rules regarding knockdowns in that the fallen fighter would have 10 seconds to rise under his own power. His opponent would have to be moved to a neutral corner before the count would be started by the referee.

The match was another 10-rounder and from all accounts

Tunney, as in their first fight, dominated the first six rounds. However in round seven the 104,943 fans would witness something that would forever be etched in history. Dempsey cornered Tunney and unleashed a series of blows which included two rights and lefts that staggered the champion and at least four more punches that knocked Tunney to the canvas. It was the first time he had hit the deck in his career. Tunney grabbed the top rope but Dempsey apparently forgetting the new rule stood in the nearest corner ready to go back into the attack should Tunney get up. The referee Dave Barry ordered Dempsey to a neutral corner and some say it took anywhere from 3 to 8 seconds before Barry was finally able to start the count. At the official count of nine Tunney got up and got on his bike. Dempsey could not catch him with a solid punch the rest of the round.

In the eighth round Tunney was once again boxing from a distance and landed a good punch to floor Dempsey. Ironically, although Jack was up almost immediately, the referee never made any attempt to guide Tunney to a neutral corner. The rest of the fight was all Tunney as he retained his title. Jack Dempsey never fought again.

In interviews over the years Gene Tunney always maintained his was aware of what was going on during the count. He claimed he could have gotten up earlier but wanted to take the full time to clear his head. The available footage of the fight even has a stopwatch super imposed on the screen showing that by the time referee Barry started the count five seconds had gone by.

Nobody will ever know for sure whether or not had Jack

Dempsey remembered the new rule and immediately gone to the farthest neutral corner, if Gene Tunney would have been able to get up or been counted out. Obviously history would have really been different had Tunney been knocked out. Jack Dempsey would have been the first heavyweight to ever regain the title (something Floyd Patterson accomplished in 1960) and who knows what would have happened after that.

Jack Dempsey certainly was one of the best heavyweights in history and how high anyone ranks him is a topic for discussion on websites and in barrooms. No doubt Jack Dempsey's career was one of controversy in so many ways. His second fight with Gene Tunney was something that I have always loved viewing and talking about. There is no right or wrong when talking about it. It is what it is—a special moment in boxing history. Forever it has been known as *"The Long Count"*.

Jack Dempsey (author's collection).

14

JERSEY JOE WALCOTT-ROCKY MARCIANO I
SEPTEMBER 23, 1952 (PHILADELPHIA)

One of the first fighters I ever really took notice of was Jersey Joe Walcott. Although I did not see him fight live I remember seeing photos of his face being distorted out of shape by Rocky Marciano's sledgehammer right hand.

As I got a little older I read more about Walcott's career and his fight with Marciano that lifted the title from him. Catching a punch landing on impact is every photographers dream. It caught my attention for sure.

Jersey Joe Walcott of course won the heavyweight championship at what was then considered a ripe old age of 37. Back then a guy like Walcott was considered ancient in boxing terms. A few of his monikers were "Pappy" because he had a large family but also "Old man Walcott".

I had the pleasure of meeting Jersey Joe for the first time in 1964 when he was a guest referee at one of Larry Atkin's last fight shows in Cleveland. He worked as a referee on the undercard. In the main event Joey Giardello, then middleweight champ, fought a non-title fight against Rocky Rivero. At the intermission I was able to meet Jersey Joe and he gave me an address in Camden, New Jersey, where I could write to him. From that we struck up a friendship and eventually met up several times, in Washington, D.C., Toronto, Canada, Los Angeles and Rochester, New York.

I also viewed many of Walcott's fights on film and then video. I was amazed at his style, his footwork, his shuffle, how he would walk away from an opponent and then turn quickly and fire a right hand. Although he didn't have a great knockout record, he did pack a potent punch in either hand. He knocked out Ezzard Charles with one dynamite left hook, had Joe Louis on the deck three times, floored Marciano and was always dangerous with either hand.

Jersey Joe won the title against Ezzard Charles on July 18, 1951, in his fifth attempt to win the title. He had previously lost two fights (although one can be debated) to Joe Louis in quest of the title and then lost two attempts to win the title against Ezzard Charles, one being in a unification bout with Ezzard when Joe Louis retired. Finally he won the title from Charles in Pittsburgh with one wicked left hook, then defended it the following June with a 15-rd decision against Charles.

Rocky Marciano was the son of Italian immigrants and lived in Brockton, Massachusetts where many of the Italians worked in the shoe factories that were so prominent in the area. Rocky wanted more. He also dreamed of being a major league catcher. However boxing caught his interest and although he officially lost four amateur fights, he caught the eye of local trainers and eventually manager Al Weill who turned him over to former fighter Charlie Goldman. Goldman turned Rocky's crude abilities into practical skills. It has been said that nobody trained harder than Rocky. His short stature and limited reach had to be overcome with boxing ability and means to get in close. Once that was accomplished his big punches would usually take care of business.

Rocky worked his way up the ladder defeating all of the contenders and near-contenders including: Phil Muscato, Roland LaStarza, Gino Buonvino, Johnny Shkor, Rex Layne, Lee Savold and Harry Kid Matthews. Also in the climb to the title he knocked out former champion, Joe Louis in the 8th round on October 26, 1951. Rocky did his job but didn't feel great about it. Louis retired for good after the bout.

When the young Rocco Francis Marchegiano, aka Rocky Marciano was given a title shot against Jersey Joe, the champion was quite outspoken and was quoted as saying he felt Marciano wasn't much, was an amateur and if he didn't defeat him that they should take his name out of the record book.

Both men had interesting backgrounds and family history. As I said Rocky was the son of Italian immigrants. Jersey Joe, real name Arnold Raymond Cream came from a tough upbringing and during his career he had many starts and stops because he had to feed his large family. He often couldn't afford to train and many of his early losses may have very well been contributed to the fact he wasn't eating right or training correctly.

When I started collecting fight films, first in 8mm, later in 16mm, one of the first fights I wanted to own was the first Walcott-Marciano fight. Over the years I have watched that fight countless times on film, later on video and DVD. It has become one of my favorite fights to view.

There has often been debate as to whether Rocky Marciano was a great fighter or not. His 49-0 record is a standard but outside of most Italian-Americans, some experts feel Rocky only fought old men, past their prime and never really defeated anyone near their prime. However no matter how you slice it, Rocky could take punishment and could punch. In that, Jersey Joe may have underestimated Marciano.

Watching the fight over the years it was obvious Jersey Joe didn't think highly of Rocky heading into the match. He tore into him from the start, hurting him and staggering him, then finally flooring him with a perfectly timed left hook. Rocky got up at either a count of two or three, depending whose view you listen to. It was give and take from that point on during round one.

The fight was a very good fight, perhaps to a degree a great fight. For the most part it was an action fight with much drama, including both men being cut and Marciano being temporarily blinded possibly by some agent used to stem either Walcott's cut over his left eye or Rocky's head wound. Other critics claim Walcott's handlers put some sort of liniment on his body.

My Favorite Fights

Both men were hit with hard punches during the match, even stunned. Carefully watching the fight, it is clear that heading into the 13th round, Jersey Joe was winning the fight and basically only had to stay on his feet to retain his title. Of course it did not happen.

During interviews over the years Rocky Marciano often said Jersey Joe gave him his greatest fight. "Old Man" or not Jersey Joe could box and punch. Who knows how boxing history would have turned out had he not been beat to the punch in that fateful 13th round.

Here is the actual ringside account of the first and thirteenth rounds by the famed Don Dunphy.

ROUND ONE

Thank you, Harry Curran. Good evening, everyone. They get out (several words missing due to sound failure) wide with a left hand. They go into a clinch. Marciano tries a left to the body. It's short. And referee Charlie Daggert goes over and gets them apart. Marciano, missing a left hand, goes into a clinch. And the big apple is on the line down here at Municipal Stadium in Philadelphia. They're still on the inside. Walcott is slow with a right hand to the chin. Now they're at long range. Walcott misses with a right over the head; it grazed the hair. In close, Walcott chops a right to the head, brings it to the body. Marciano tries to tie him up in the inside. Most of the milling is in close. At long range Walcott lands with a jab, puts a right on the face, misses a right, crosses a right, chops away with two more rights to the head, bangs both hands to the body, crosses a right to the jaw. Marciano mainly trying to tie him up for a moment, moves his way into a clinch. And Walcott is throwing heavily here in round one. Marciano rips a long right hand to the body, crosses a right to the jaw. Marciano is hurt, with a left and right to the head by Walcott as they clinch over in Marciano's corner. Two minutes to go. And Marciano is down by a left hook on the chin. He takes a two-count and he's up. Marciano was down by a left hook. Walcott on top of him again with another left hook, rips a right to the head, misses a left jab. Marciano goes in and holds on for a moment and Walcott was within a few seconds of victory. Walcott misses a left hand over the head, and there they are in a clinch again. Now they're are at long range. Walcott takes a light right and a long right hand to the head thrown by Marciano. In close. Half the round is gone. Marciano gets away from a right, smashes a right to the jaw and hurts Walcott. And Walcott may have let him get away. Now they're at long range again. Marciano has recovered from the early battering. He takes a solid left hook on the jaw by Walcott, a right high on the head, and Walcott is in trying for a quick knockout if he possibly can. At long range, Marciano makes Walcott miss, drives a left and right to the jaw and takes a right chop high on the head by the champion, Jersey Joe Walcott. One minute to go in round one now. Walcott crosses a right hand to the jaw. Marciano, as you know was down for about a two-count. Now they're at long range again. Walcott, working his way in, takes a sold right hand to the jaw, a light right hand to the body by Marciano. Now they're in close again and the referee is getting them apart. At long range, Walcott comes back with a left to the head, moves in close, and Marciano ties him up on the inside. It's been a rocky round for the challenger so far. He takes a solid left hook to the jaw and throws his own right hand to the head as Walcott comes in on him. They're in close again. Now at long range. Marciano misses a left over the head, takes a right chop a couple of times to the body by Walcott. In a clinch. Out of it again. Parted by referee Charlie Daggert. Walcott misses a right over the head, misses a left, and Marciano has gone into a crouching style and on the inside chops a short right to the jaw. A right to the head and a right and left to the jaw by Marciano. After Walcott had scored first, Marciano comes back with solid thumps to the head. Marciano digs a left hand to the body. They're in a clinch just above us now. Walcott backs away to the center of the ring and now they tie each other up on the inside and this round is almost over. (Sound of bell) There's the bell.

ROUND THIRTEEN

Marciano has been in trouble the last couple of rounds, but he gets out there quickly and moves in on Walcott, who paws out with a left hand to the body. It's short. Marciano is short with a left jab aimed at the head. Marciano digs a left hand to the pit of the stomach of Walcott, Walcott backing away now. Here's Marciano moving in on him again, Walcott feinting the left hand, going into a shuffle, Marciano bulling his way in close. Walcott's ageless legs keep taking him back out of trouble whenever he gets into it. Marciano bulling his way in close. Walcott is back to the ropes. Takes a right to the jaw. Walcott is staggered and helpless on the ropes, with a right to the jaw. Walcott is down on his stomach and they're counting over him. It may be a knockout. I don't think Walcott can get up. It's going to be a knockout for Marciano. Rocky Marciano by a knockout. A straight right-hand punch to the jaw. And Walcott rolls over. He is still out cold. It is a knockout, and we have a new heavyweight champion of the world. It is Rocky Marciano, still undefeated, from Brockton, Massachusetts.

The Author with Jersey Joe Walcott (Author's collection).

15

JOE LOUIS-BILLY CONN I
JUNE 18, 1941 (NEW YORK)

There are certain fights that always come to mind when thinking of some of the great fights or at least most memorable fights from the glory days of boxing. Usually when asked, most knowledgeable historians and fans immediately blurt out several including Dempsey-Tunney, Zale-Graziano, Ali-Frazier and quite often Louis-Conn.

I had read about the two bouts between Joe Louis and Billy Conn long before I actually got to see them on film. Of course the second fight never approached greatness. The first encounter in June of 1941 was historic for many reasons. I loved watching the film of the first fight and never guessed that someday I would meet Billy Conn and get to spend time with him.

In the late 70s, early 80s I was involved with an organization called The Rochester Boxing Association. Later it would be called The Rochester Boxing Hall of Fame. This upstate

New York group started in 1978. I got involved with them and began attending the dinners each year.

Because I had a reputation of having met several former champions and contenders I was asked if I could possibly invite some of these former champs to the Rochester Boxing Association annual awards banquet. I was fortunate to get Tony Zale and Jimmy Bivins as their honored guests for their 1979 event. The following year, 1980, I landed Jimmy McLarnin and Jersey Joe Walcott. I was able to get those two great fighters to come because I had already met them and developed a regular friendship with them for a number of years. In the case of Jimmy McLarnin I had known him since 1975, and I had first met Jersey Joe Walcott in 1964 and we kept in touch over the years.

Prior to 1980 I had never had the opportunity to meet Billy Conn even though he only lived around 130 miles from Cleveland in Pittsburgh. As fate would have it I met Billy Conn's oldest son Tim. I don't remember who contacted who first but Tim was working as a sales rep for a manufacturing company based in Cleveland. He came to Cleveland from Pittsburgh on business at least once a month. I invited him to visit with me and my family and it became a regular happening most months when he came to Cleveland. Sometimes we would have dinner at our house, other times we would go to a little local spot of which Tim became very fond. Of course I picked Tim's brain about his famous dad. You could tell how proud he was to have Billy Conn as his father. He had so many interesting and funny stories.

My relationship with Tim led me to ask him if his father

would like to be one of the honored guests for the 1981 dinner in Rochester. Billy accepted and along with Earnie Shavers, another fighter I had a friendship with going back to 1973, they became the two honorees at the Rochester Boxing Association awards banquet that year.

During the weekend in Rochester I met up with Billy Conn and his lovely wife, Mary Louise in their hotel room prior to the dinner. I found Billy to be open and frank about most everything we discussed. To say he didn't "pull any punches" would be an understatement. I felt like I had known him for years and he didn't fail to respond to any question I asked and certainly wasn't shy about giving an opinion. He was straight forward and funny and just a delight to talk to. Sometimes his wife would just shake her head when he used colorful language to talk about an event that happened during his career. He sat there on his bed, a casual setting to say the least.

The 1981 dinner was a big success and those in attendance were thrilled to meet Billy Conn. Highlights of the first Louis-Conn fight were shown and Billy had many humorous anecdotes about the fight. Thankfully this was not my last encounter with Billy Conn. He came back to Rochester a couple more times. A few years after that first dinner Tim Conn invited me to come to Pittsburgh for a weekend because Billy Conn and some other star Pittsburgh sports personalities were being honored at a big event. During that trip, although I stayed with Tim Conn and his family, I was also able to visit Billy and Mary Louise at their beautiful home in the Squirrel Hill section of Pittsburgh. That was a special time and most rewarding. I saw Billy's game room where many famous photos and awards covered the walls. Billy hung out with many celebrities during his career and after. I saw photos of he and Bob Hope and other Hollywood stars adorning the walls. Most of all it was another opportunity to ask Billy more questions and just listen to his stories.

I am sure most people who have any grasp of boxing history know about the actual fight that took place in 1941 between Billy Conn and Joe Louis. The younger and much lighter Conn put on a boxing clinic. He jabbed in and out, threw left hooks and stayed out of the reach of Louis' big counter punches. Louis at the weigh-in was just a little under 200 lbs. Conn was listed at 174 lbs. However Billy always maintained that he only weighed 169 lbs. but that Mike Jacobs the promoter was afraid people would be up in arms if they listed him at such a light weight so they made it sound a little better.

Joe Louis was listed an 11-5 favorite. The crowd at The Polo Grounds in New York was 54,487 and the gate as $452,743. Louis got 40% and Conn 17 ½%. There are various versions about the fight including statements that Billy Conn had the fight won when he got knocked out and would have won had he just lasted the fifteen rounds. Although he was ahead on two of the scorecards, it was even on the third. Referee Eddie Joseph had Conn ahead 7-5, judge Marty Monroe had it 7-4-1 Conn and judge Bill Healy had it even at 6-6. So technically Conn could have still lost the fight on a decision. He needed to win one of the last three rounds to assure the victory.

Of course history will always show and no matter how many times you watch the film, a decision wasn't going to determine the result. Billy had hurt and staggered Louis in the twelfth round and the story most often discussed is that Conn decided he was going to finish off Louis. It was said that he told his corner he was going out to finish Louis and that they pleaded with him to box and not trade with Louis. It has always been said that Billy let his Irish temper get the better of him. He was always a tough, cocky kind of guy. He had no fear and a ton of confidence. I don't doubt that Billy felt he could knock Louis out. He almost made it through the round but Louis hurt Conn with a right hand and didn't let him off the hook. Louis to me was one of the greatest finishers ever in the heavyweight ranks, if not the best. A series of lefts and rights sent Conn to the canvas where he was counted out at 2:58 of the round.

If he had survived those last few seconds, would he have come to his senses and stayed away and boxed the next two rounds? We will never know. I was told by Billy personally that he had visited his mother in the hospital prior to the fight. She was gravely ill and Billy said, "Ma the next time you see me I will be heavyweight champion of the world". Billy told me that his statement after the fight, "I guess I had too much to win for tonight, otherwise I would have won easy", was referring to what he had said to his mother.

Billy Conn and Joe Louis met up many times over the years. I am not even going to discuss their return match in 1946, after both of them served in WWII. It wasn't much of a fight and both men had lost a lot of their greatness. Over the years they often found themselves at boxing dinners and other events. They became good friends and had much respect for each other. One of the funniest stories is how at one event their first fight was being shown on a big movie screen in a theater. Just before the 13th round started Joe Louis headed up toward the exit. Billy supposedly said, "Hey Joe where are you going?" According to Billy Conn Joe said, "I've seen this Billy, I know how it ends."

Billy also would tell another story at most dinners or even in private. He claims sometime after the fight he ran into Joe Louis and said to him. "Hey Joe why couldn't you have let me win the title, I could have kept it for six months and then let you win it back" or words pretty close to that. Supposedly Joe said to Billy, "Hell Billy you had it for twelve rounds and couldn't keep it, how would you have kept it for six months?".

The Author with Pittsburgh's Billy Conn (author's collection).

16

JOE LOUIS-JERSEY JOE WALCOTT I
DECEMBER 5, 1947 (NEW YORK)

Without a doubt I have always felt that Joe Louis is one of the top two heavyweight champions in history. Critics will say he fought bums but in reality he fought everyone that was available, he met all comers. To defend your title twenty-five times and to hold that crown for eleven years is an amazing feat that nobody should ever dispute. The few opponents who managed to give a good account of themselves when they met Joe Louis the first time probably would have been a lot wiser not to seek a return match. Louis was deadly in those bouts.

Jersey Joe Walcott on the other hand had a rocky road to a title fight and eventually the heavyweight crown. He had several periods during his career where he had to take time off and work other jobs. It has often been said that he was under-fed and under-trained during those early years. Besides losing to fighters such as Henry Taylor, Billy Ketchell, George Brothers and Roy Lazer, he was also stopped by Al

Ettore, Tiger Jack Fox and Abe Simon as he tried to move up into heavyweight contention. Usually the fight reports seemed to indicate he had run out of gas in many of these matches. But in the late 1940s Jersey Joe changed management and finally started to get the proper training he sometimes had lacked.

Cleveland's Jimmy Bivins had been at the top or near the top of the rankings in two divisions for most of the 1940s. When he and Jersey Joe finally met on February 25, 1946, in Cleveland, Jimmy Bivins was riding a 27-bout unbeaten streak. Jimmy Bivins once told me that at the time they met "Jersey Joe wasn't even the picture or considered a top contender". Looking at his record for 1945 I find that a little hard to imagine because Jersey Joe had won eight out of nine fights that year including wins over Joe Baksi and Lee Q Murray. He also had a big stoppage over Curtis "Hatchetman" Sheppard in the 10th round. Still when Jimmy Bivins and Jersey Joe Walcott clashed at the Cleveland Arena the smart money was on Bivins. In the end Jersey Joe won a split decision which in itself was odd because the official scoring had Jimmy on top of two of the judge's cards. Judge Tony LaBranch had it 9-1 for Walcott; however, referee Jackie Davis had it 6-4 for Bivins. Judge Charlie Bill, although scoring it for Bivins in rounds 5-4-1, gave the match to Walcott because he had floored Bivins in the 7th round. This win by Jersey Joe made many sit up and take notice. It ended Bivins' win streak and was considered a very important victory for Jersey Joe.

Later in 1946 Jersey Joe dropped two decisions, one to Joey Maxim and the other to Elmer "Violent" Ray. To some he may have seemed to be fading from contention once again. But then he defeated both men in return matches and defeated Maxim a second time in June.

I have often read that when the proposed fight between Joe Louis and Jersey Joe Walcott was first talked about the promoters were trying to have them fight an exhibition. Somehow more rational minds prevailed and the match was set as a regular 15-round title defense for Louis. Although the great Joe Louis was nearing the end of his long reign most experts didn't give ol' Jersey Joe much of a chance to defeat Louis or even last the distance. Heading into their match according to my records Jersey Joe had a so-so record of 46-11-1 while Louis had a spectacular mark of 54-1 with 46 knockouts. Louis was established a 10-1 favorite in most betting.

I have watched a lot of Joe Louis fights on film. I am always amazed at his accuracy in punching with either hand and till this day I feel he was one of the greatest finishers in boxing history. Once he got you hurt it was just a matter of time. He could hurt you with a jab, a left hook or a right hand. His combinations were swift and accurate. As a puncher Louis really didn't have any weaknesses. Critics say that he was too slow and methodical of foot to defeat someone as swift and mobile as the young Muhammad Ali. That is good for boxing forums and debates but it doesn't matter, to me Joe Louis was very, very special.

Jersey Joe Walcott when at his best was also a very special fighter. One can only watch in awe at his movement in the ring. He was unique, especially with his footwork and his trick of appearing to walk away from an opponent and then suddenly turning back to launch a right hand. Both Louis and Walcott were born in 1914 and actually Jersey Joe was a few months older than the champ. Louis and others always felt that Walcott might have been even a few years older than listed. Back then athletes, especially boxers were consider old at age 33. But while Joe Louis seemed to be reaching the end of the line to many Jersey Joe perhaps was just reaching his best days.

The fight itself drew 18,194 fans at Madison Square Garden in New York. Louis tipped the scales at 211 ½ lbs. while Jersey Joe weighed in at 194 ½, a normal weight for him. Referee was Ruby Goldstein. The first round started out with both men boxing smartly. Around midway into the round Louis got Walcott into a corner and both men exchanged punches. Louis appeared to be teeing off on Walcott but seeing the sequence later in slow motion it was obvious that Jersey Joe either slipped or rolled with most of the punches, that none landed cleanly. Then Jersey landed a good right hand and dumped Louis. He was up quickly and didn't appear to be hurt. Walcott couldn't land anymore big punches the rest of the round.

In the second round it appeared Louis was stalking Walcott, and Jersey Joe did land a couple very solid countering right hands. Walcott as always was doing his shuffle, his shoulder roll, his stepping away and turning back. Todays' fans would be amazed that a full- fledged heavyweight like Walcott could move the way he did.

In the next two rounds the script continued. Jersey Joe behind a left jab and his good movement in my mind was putting on a boxing clinic. In round four Louis shuffled in and got belted with a very good right hand that deposited him on his rear end once again. This time he did not pop up, rather got up in a position to hear the count and take it while his head cleared before getting upright. As the rounds went by the fight pretty much stayed the same. Walcott would use his jab, move around, stepping out of harm's way. Louis did land occasional hard punches but never in combinations. Jersey Joe never seemed to be in any serious trouble.

According to fight reports and upon watching this fight over again my feelings are that heading into the last three rounds of the fight Jersey Joe could have safely claimed eight of those rounds. Back then great champions like Joe Louis were often given the benefit of the doubt in close rounds. At least that is my opinion. So although Jersey Joe fought a very clever, smart fight, some later would say he should have been more aggressive in the last three rounds of the fight and that is what cost him the verdict.

When the final bell sounded and before any announcement could be made Joe Louis is seen ducking through the ropes getting ready to leave the ring. That was and is interpreted as Joe Louis admitting defeat and wanting to get out of there. Years later on talk shows he claimed he knew he didn't fight a good fight but felt he won.

When the scorecards were read one judge, Frank Forbes had it 8-6-1 for Louis, the other judge, Marty Monroe had it 9-6 Louis and only referee Ruby Goldstein favored Walcott with a score of 7-6-2. Watching the film you can see total disbelief from Walcott's corner. One corner man is seen raising his hands in the air, the other slapping his hands to his head several times. The crowd gave Jersey Joe a long standing ovation. A poll of 32 boxing writers had 21 voting for Walcott, 10 for Louis with one calling it a draw.

Jersey Joe would get a return match in 1948, even flooring Louis one more time. He put up another great effort until Louis caught up with him in round eleven with several beautiful combinations, knocking him down and Jersey Joe could not beat the count. Till this day many historians including me feel the fight between these two men in 1947 will always rank as a classic bad decision.

17

JOE LOUIS-MAX SCHMELING II
JUNE 22, 1938 (NEW YORK)

The second Joe Louis-Max Schmeling fight is one of the most historic fights ever. Due to the circumstances and time in history it had much more significance than a normal heavyweight fight. As the war in Europe was getting nearer Germany and the insane leadership of Adolf Hitler were spouting propaganda about their "Superior Race".

The Nazis officially came into power in 1933. On June 19, 1936 Max Schmeling perhaps the best fighter to ever come out of Germany, met the undefeated "Brown" Bomber" Joe Louis in New York. He scored a huge upset when he stopped Louis in the 12th round. Schmeling would be held up as an example of Germany's superior racial theories and he became a huge hero back home. Prior to the fight Max had stated that he saw something in Louis, a flaw as it was. It turned out as he was watching footage of Louis' previous fights he noticed that Louis was dropping his left hand.

During the 1936 fight he was able to hit Joe with right hands over his left leads fairly easily.

Joe Louis worked his way back into contention after the Schmeling defeat with eleven straight victories including knockouts over former champion, Jack Sharkey, Al Ettore, Cleveland's Eddie Simms and Natie Brown. He also defeated tough contender Bob Pastor by decision.

On June 22, 1937 Joe Louis met James J Braddock for the heavyweight title. After hitting the deck himself he came back to stop the courageous champion in the 8th round. The Joe Louis era as champion had begun. He would then defend his title three times in 1937 and 1938. The Welshman Tommy Farr gave him a spirited fight and lasted the 15-round distance. Louis then knocked out Nathan Mann in the 3rd round and Harry Thomas in the 5th.

Joe Louis was not satisfied however. He was quoted as saying he would never feel like he was the real champion until he avenged his defeat against Max Schmeling. It may have been a matter of pride on Joe's part. Many American fans saw the return match differently. They felt Louis would show the world he was the better man in every way. Just as Schmeling was being used in Germany's propaganda machine, in some ways Joe Louis would become a symbol for all that was right in the free world. Although World War II did not officially start until September of 1939, when Louis and Schmeling were signed for the rematch on June 22, 1938, more than boxing fans were watching.

There isn't a whole lot I can add to the actual fight itself. This is the shortest fight on my list of favorites and it showed

My Favorite Fights

Joe Louis at his lethal best. Max Schmeling never had a chance and when the fight was stopped in the first round it was to save Max from further injury. His corner tried to stop the fight. Trainer Max Machon tried to throw in the towel as a sign of surrender. This was common in European fights but had not been adopted in the USA. Referee Arthur Donovan tossed the towel aside and started the count. But at five he realized it was hopeless and stopped the contest. The time was 2:04.

When Louis first hurt Max he caught him near the ropes and landed a series of shots to both the head and the body. Max was turned sideways as he hung onto the ropes and took several shots to his back and kidney area. His legs dipped but he never went down so referee Donovan signaled the men to continue fighting. There was nothing illegal about what Louis did. Max instinctively tried to turn away from the assault and the flurry of punches being thrown by Joe Louis landed most everywhere including his backside as he turned around.

After the fight Max Schmeling had to go to the hospital. It was revealed that he had two fractures to his back and other injuries. It was one of the most dynamic knockouts in modern boxing history. 70,043 watched the fight live at Yankee Stadium and millions listened to it on the radio.

I have watched this short fight many times. When I was still in my 20s I used to go to a nightclub that had television monitors in the corners of the main floor. They showed short clips of famous sporting events in a constant loop and two of those were highlights of the Louis-Schmeling fights. I watched them over and over during the times I visited that establishment.

Max Schmeling's career basically was over after the second Louis fight although he did win the European Heavyweight Title over Adolf Heuser in July of 1939. By the time the war started in September of 1939, Schmeling had fallen out of favor with the German hierarchy and ended up serving as a common soldier, a paratrooper in Crete where he was injured. There was never any real proof that Schmeling was ever an official member of the Nazi party. He had a handful of fights after the war with mixed results. For a time after the war he was not allowed to enter the United States. Later it was proven that he never was guilty of any war crimes or illegal activities and he was allowed to come to America. He and Joe Louis became very good friends and Max visited Joe several times. Max became a successful businessman with a Coca Cola Distributorship in Germany. It was written that he paid for many of Louis' bills when Joe came upon hard times in his later years. Max may have even paid for Joe Louis' funeral in 1981.

Boxing certainly has shown over the years that even though men can beat each other senseless in the ring, that outside of the ring they can also be the best of friends. Max and Joe never let the politics of the world nor their rivalry in the ring come between them as human beings.

Joe Louis and Max Schmeling (author's collection).

Joey Giardello (left) on the way to defeating Rocky Rivero (author's collection).

18

JOEY GIARDELLO-ROCKY RIVERO

APRIL 17, 1964 AND MAY 22, 1964 (CLEVELAND, OHIO)

I was fortunate to witness Joey Giardello fight live three different times during my early days of following boxing. The first time was on November 4, 1959, when Joey defeated Dick Tiger by decision over ten rounds. The other two fights occurred within a month of each other in the Spring of 1964. All three were held at the old Cleveland Arena at East 37th and Euclid Avenue.

As are a few other fights I write about in this book I am sure the two Giardello-Rivero contests in 1964 more than likely will never go down historically as classic bouts. However they were good action fights and because I witnessed them live they will always hold special memories for me, not only for the action in the ring but for other events that transpired outside of the ropes.

It is hard for me to separate the two fights because they were similar in many ways. Although Joey Giardello was middleweight champion at the time, (when I think back about it now) Giardello was nearing the end of his long and illustrious career. Both of the Rivero fights saw him forced to use all of his skill and toughness to overcome his rampaging opponent. Both bouts were close and saw Joey take a lot of punishment at times but also use his boxing skills to pull out the verdicts. The first bout on April 17th was the closer of the two with referee Tony La Branch scoring it 46-45 for Joey as did judge Bill Thompson. Judge Charley Bill scored it 46-45 for Rivero. There was scattered booing when the fight ended as some in attendance felt Rivero had done enough to win the decision.

When the scorecards were tallied after the May 22nd return match, referee Mike Minnich called it 46-43 for Giardello, judge Herb Williams scored it 45-44 for Joey and judge Bill Thompson had it 46-45 for the champion. Joey always called Cleveland "His lucky town" as he was 7-0 here throughout his career.

Besides the obvious fact that I realized at a very young age that I liked boxing a lot, you might say I loved it, I also knew that seeing a world champion, even in non-title fights was something special. We didn't have an abundance of world champions fighting in Cleveland as the 1960s went along. The two Giardello-Rivero fights also were special for me in another very important way. Larry Atkins who probably will go down in history as certainly one of the best ever Cleveland matchmakers/promoters if not the best, put on some of the greatest fights in the history of our city. Besides bringing in Joey Giardello two more times, he also had some of the best fighters in history scheduled as guests or guest referees.

My Favorite Fights

Attending these two Giardello-Rivero fights allowed me to meet the following fighters for the very first and in some cases only time. I met Joe Louis, Ezzard Charles, Jersey Joe Walcott, Jimmy Bivins, Rocky Marciano, Rocky Graziano and Joey Giardello. Graziano worked the corner of Rivero and Marciano worked the corner of Giardello. Both Louis and Walcott were refs for the under-card at the second fight.

Joey Giardello had a long and successful career. Over the years I read many articles about him and some writers liked to write about a lot more information than just his wins and losses. Joey had been involved in various forms of trouble outside of the ring and had even served time in prison. He also had at least two rather controversial fights during his career where the scoring was changed after the fight. The first one was on December 19, 1952, when Joey won a split decision over the very talented Billy Graham in New York. After the fight Boxing Commissioners Robert Christenberry and CB Powell altered one of the judges cards to change the verdict to a win for Graham. The original cards had referee Ray Miller scoring it 5-4-1 for Giardello and judge Joe Agnello having it 6-4 for Joey. Judge Charley Shortell had it 7-3 for Graham. The Commissioners changed Agnello's card. Giardello took it all the way to the New York Supreme Court and the court reversed the reversal, once again giving Giardello his rightful decision win.

The second crazy bout happened on March 25, 1957, in Kansas City, Missouri. After the fight between Giardello and

Willie Vaughn, the fight was announced as a split decision win for Vaughn. The fight was supposed to be scored on the five-point must system, but referee Ray Sissom inadvertently used the 10-point scoring system. The Missouri Athletic Commission later declared his card invalid and ordered the contest recorded as a no-decision.

When Joey finally got a title shot against Gene Fullmer in 1960, he had been campaigning almost thirteen years. He and Gene Fullmer met in Bozeman, Montana on April 20, 1960, and it turned out to be a dirty affair with both fighters butting the other numerous times. The fight was called a draw. Till their deaths both men blamed the other one for starting the butting. It was obvious they did not like each other.

Joey Giardello continued on with his career and eventually after winning some important fights, including a decision over Sugar Ray Robinson, he was awarded a second title shot. This time he left no doubt as he took a clear cut 15-round decision over champion, Dick Tiger and won all of the marbles on December 7, 1963, in Atlantic City.

As champion he had the two non-title Rivero bouts and eventually defended his crown against Rubin "Hurricane" Carter in his hometown of Philadelphia. Although portrayed later in the movie "The Hurricane" as a decision that robbed Carter of the title, in reality Joey won the decision fair and square. He later sued the makers of the movie in court and won an undisclosed amount.

On October 21, 1965, Joey lost the title to Dick Tiger by a lopsided decision and after four more fights retired for good. In 134 fights he won 101, while only losing 25 with 7 draws and that one no-decision contest. He was entered into the Philadelphia Sports Hall of Fame, The World Boxing Hall of Fame and The International Boxing Hall of Fame. A statue of Joey is situated in the East Passyunk Crossing section of South Philadelphia.

The author with heavyweight champion Larry Holmes (author's collection).

19

KEN NORTON-LARRY HOLMES

JUNE 9, 1978 (LAS VEGAS)

One of the heavyweight fights from the 70s that is talked about often is the battle between Ken Norton and Larry Holmes. Their fight took place in 1978 during the time 15-round championship bouts were still in vogue. I often see fans on Facebook say that this fight was their favorite.

The meeting between these two came about because one of the alphabet groups as I have always referred to them, the WBC (World Boxing Council) decided to have a heavyweight eliminator between Ken Norton and Jimmy Young. When Norton won the 15-round fight on November 5, 1977 he was declared the outstanding challenger for Leon Spink's world title. Spinks won the title in a huge upset over Muhammad Ali on February 15, 1978, in Las Vegas. When Spinks decided to give Ali a return match rather than fight Norton the WBC stripped Spinks of the title and proclaimed that Ken Norton was WBC World Champion, even though he never won the actual title in the ring. Norton probably is best known during his career for having three very close battles with Muhammad Ali. Many fans and experts felt he won at least two of their fights although he was only given the decision in their first match on March 31, 1973 in San Diego. It was during that fight that Muhammad Ali suffered a broken jaw.

It was decided that Ken Norton would defend his newly appointed title against Larry Holmes. He had a fine record of 40-4 with 32 knockouts. He had been stopped twice himself. Ken Norton, a former Marine fought out of San Diego. Larry Holmes was an undefeated heavyweight out of Easton, Pa. He had won 27 straight fights with his biggest win being a 12-round lopsided decision over Earnie Shavers on March 25, 1978 in Las Vegas. He had scored 19 knockouts.

Don King matched these two fine fighters on June 9, 1978, in Las Vegas. Ken Norton was established a 6-5 favorite heading into the fight. He weighed in at 220 lbs. Larry Holmes was 209 lbs. It was stated more than once that they did not like each other. Whether it was hype or real feelings I do not know.

During the instructions by referee Mills Lane, Norton and Holmes bumped into each other and stood nose to nose at times. You could feel the energy, that these two were ready to battle. It was looking to be a special fight and that is the way it turned out. But in the beginning it did not appear it would go that way because Larry Holmes started quickly and Ken Norton couldn't seem to get untracked. Later on Ken Norton would admit that it was a critical mistake. Holmes won four of the first five rounds easily, mainly because of his left jab.

My Favorite Fights

In round six Ken Norton finally stepped up the pace and shook Larry Holmes with a big right hand. In round seven he changed his attack to the body. After the fight Larry Holmes said that he got hit on the left bicep and for a while he felt that it went dead on him.

Ken Norton won five of the next six rounds which made the fight very even. Both men were showing fatigue from the fast pace they had set. Holmes' jab came back into play. Throughout his pro career the one punch that often set Larry aside from others was his jab. Holmes won the 12th and the 13th, staggering Norton at least twice with right hands.

The warriors were pretty much spent as they came out for the 14th. But Ken Norton went to the well and forced himself to take the fight to Holmes. By far he had the better of the round, landing many good punches to the head and body. This set up a fantastic finish.

The 15th round was going to determine the outcome of the fight. Norton started strong and was throwing all kinds of punches, jabbing, hooking. Blood was pouring out of Holmes' mouth from a cut inside his lower lip that happened several rounds earlier. After the fight it would take eleven stitches.

Holmes began to fight back as they stood toe-to-toe. They punched on with no regard to defense. Larry Holmes took command of the round at the end and staggered Norton with a right. They barely made it back to their corners.

When the scores were read judge Harold Buck scored it 143-142 for Holmes, judge Joe Swessel also scored it 143-142 for

Holmes while judge Lou Tabat had it 143-142 for Norton. The unofficial AP scorecard had it 143-142 for Norton.

Norton was listed as receiving $2.3 million for his end of the purse while Holmes got $300,000. The sellout crowd of 5,600 at Caesars Palace loved the fight but more than a few disagreed with the verdict.

Holmes was the new WBC World Heavyweight Champion, a title he would hold until October 2, 1980, when he was given full World Champion status after defeating Muhammad Ali. He eventually lost his world title to Michael Spinks in 1985.

The Norton-Holmes fight is one frequently discussed as a fan favorite in recent heavyweight history. It has been debated over and over but the bottom line is that it was one terrific fight and most say the 15th round was one of the best rounds ever.

20

MICHAEL DOKES-GERRIE COETZEE

SEPTEMBER 23, 1983 (RICHFIELD, OHIO)

I was involved with the start up of The Parma Boxing Club outside of Cleveland in the Spring of 1979. My friends Don Myers and Dave Cass did the brunt of the work, but I joined them in other capacities for a number of years. Perhaps the two most memorable events that happened at our west side gym was when Roberto Duran trained there in 1981 for his comeback fight against Nino Gonzalez. Then in the Fall of 1983 South Africa's Gerrie Coetzee finished up his training there as he challenged Akron's Michael Dokes for the WBA Heavyweight Title that Dokes had won the year before against Mike Weaver.

Gerrie Coetzee had fought for the title twice before. He lost a 15-round decision to John Tate in Pretoria in October of 1979. He had earned that first title shot with twenty-two straight wins, including knocking out Ron Stander, Tom Prater, Johnny Boudreaux and stopping Leon Spinks in one round. Although he fought only once more after his title loss to Tate, knocking out Mike Koranicki in the first round, he was granted a second shot at the title against Mike Weaver. Weaver had won the title by stopping John Tate with a dramatic 15th round knockout in March of 1980. Gerrie's second title shot found him making a heroic effort against Weaver but he was halted in the 13th round in October of 1980, in Johannesburg.

Not giving up on his title aspirations Coetzee once again got himself back into title contention with wins over George Chaplin, a controversial decision loss to Renaldo Snipes, knockouts over Fossie Schmidt, Scott LeDoux and Stan Ward and then fought to a draw with Pinklon Thomas. Don King signed him to fight Michael Dokes for the WBA version of the heavyweight title at the beautiful Richfield Coliseum, basically between Cleveland and Akron, Ohio. This was the same venue that he staged the Muhammad Ali-Chuck Wepner fight in 1975. Leading up to the fight there were some minor protests about the policies of South Africa. Some felt it was a betrayal that a black man such as King would promote a fight between a white fighter from South Africa, a country still in the throes of Apartheid and a black American. Don King, who controlled the purse strings of Michael Dokes, could have cared less about the black-white issue. All he cared about was green, the color of money.

The Richfield Coliseum had a capacity of around 22,000 seats, but approximately 7,000 or so showed up for the fight. A large group of fans took the long trip from South Africa to support their hero, Coetzee. First they went to a Casino in Atlantic City, New Jersey, and then I personally set them up with a day at the races at our local thoroughbred track, Thistledown, in Cleveland. They even had a race named after them. Several dozen would also show up at the Parma Boxing Club to watch Gerrie Coetzee work out each day.

The fight itself was exciting, if not great. For heavyweights they set a pretty good pace. A couple days before the fight I had been asked by South African promoter Cedric Kushner whether or not I thought Gerrie could beat Michael Dokes. I am no fortune teller and I rarely gamble but I do recall telling him I felt Gerrie would need to box a bit more, not just launch right hands and he would have a good chance.

Gerrie did come out boxing in the first round and did land a good combination near the end of the round. In the second round Coetzee was attacking at the end of the round and got hit with a left hook that opened a nasty cut between the eye lid and eye brow of his right eye. Jackie McCoy, the California manager and cornerman who had guided five world champions during his career, including lightweight champs Mando Ramos and Rodolfo Gonzalez and welterweight Carlos Palamino, was utilized by Coetzee's father and South African trainer, Willie Lock to help train Gerrie for the Dokes fight. He also had a good reputation as a cut man. His skills would be needed.

The third round saw the cut opening up right away but it didn't seem to get any worse. However Gerrie seemed to be countering more, rather than attacking. He pawed at the cut, apparently it was bothering him. Jackie McCoy and the rest of the corner must have convinced Gerrie the cut was no worse as he became more aggressive in the next couple of rounds. In round five he floored Dokes to one knee with a nice counter right hand and Dokes took the eight count. Michael had a look of bewilderment on his face as he got up.

As I said the fight itself was fast paced for the most part although both fighters missed a lot of punches. The announcing team kept making references that Coetzee often ran out of gas after about eight rounds.

Michael Dokes clearly spent too much time on the ropes and the announcers constantly made reference about that too. The rounds went by and to me from my vantage point ringside I felt Coetzee was landing the better punches although Dokes did land a few good counter right hands. But they were few and far between. You could feel his title was slipping away from him.

Dokes got warned several times for low blows as he tried to go to the body. Coetzee was much more effective with his body shots. Finally in the 9th round Dokes was up on his toes and seemed to have a little more energy. But near the end of the round Coetzee landed some very hard punches and Michael seemed very tired as he headed to the corner at the bell.

Round ten started uneventfully, but suddenly as the round went along Coetzee seemed to be finding the range. He landed a good left hook near the end of the round and this set up a series of right hands that staggered Dokes. Coetzee seemed to hurry much too quickly for a moment as he rushed across the ring trying to finish Dokes off. He even hit him with an illegal backhand. Then he caught Dokes with a staggering right that sent him helpless into the ropes near a neutral corner where I was sitting, and landed two more big rights that sent Michael down face first as the round was coming to an end. The bell rang but the rules stated a fighter could not be saved by the bell so Dokes was counted out by referee Tony Perez at 3:08 of the round.

The small crowd which had that large contingent of South Africans, erupted into a roar as Coetzee fell to the canvas in utter joy as his handlers charged over to congratulate him. Donald King managed to step over the prone Dokes to rush over and hug Gerrie Coetzee after he got up. So much for loyalty.

What really surprised me was how the fight had been scored at the time of the knockout. Judge Guy Jutras had it 88-85 for Coetzee, Fernando Viso had it 87-86 for Coetzee and Samuel Conde Lopez had it 87-85 for Coetzee. I could not see Dokes winning one or two rounds at most and would have had him much further behind if I had been scoring.

In recent boxing history in Ohio and especially the Cleveland area where I live there has not been a lot of good boxing action. But I will always remember the Michael Dokes-Gerrie Coetzee fight because I had the pleasure of spending time with Gerrie at our gym and meeting some of his fans, trainers etc. Most people would have thought I would be a Michael Dokes fan because he was a local guy from Akron, Ohio. Actually I wasn't... probably because one of my good friends was a bitter rival of his in the amateurs and I never liked the way Dokes acted in the times I encountered him. Nothing personal, I just never warmed up to him as one of my favorites. That is not to say I didn't think he had a ton of talent. It is a shame he let himself get involved with drugs and alcohol, in addition to other personal problems because he really should have been on top a lot longer than he was. Michael Dokes had an excellent amateur career, winning National AAU and Golden Gloves titles. His pro career was good but perhaps could have been even great. Sadly he was only 54 years old when he died of liver cancer in 2012.

The fight was memorable for obvious reasons and the aftermath even more so. Gerrie's wife Rena went into labor after the bout and their daughter Tana was delivered on Saturday, the day after the fight at Mr. Sinai Hospital in Cleveland. Tana weighed in at 7 lbs, 12 ounces. Needless to say winning the heavyweight title and welcoming their third child into this world was something Gerrie and Rena would never forget.

The end is near as challenger Gerrie Coetzee staggers champion, Michael Dokes on the ropes. (Photo-Terry Gallagher)

Ali finishes off Wepner in the 15th round (Plain Dealer).

21

MUHAMMAD ALI-CHUCK WEPNER

MARCH 24, 1975 (RICHFIELD, OHIO)

Memorable fights are not always classic fights as I have said. But during the wonderful era of the 70s any fight with Muhammad Ali involved had to be memorable for one reason or another. I didn't have a lot of opportunities to see Muhammad fight, so when the match was signed for him to defend against Chuck Wepner of New Jersey I was more than grateful to be able to attend and cover it for a couple magazines.

Most of the live fight cards I was able to attend in the 1970s and early 1980s in Cleveland I sat ringside in the Press Row. For whatever reason for the Ali-Wepner fight I was given a Roving Photographers Pass. I was not a professional photographer back then nor am I now. However I have captured a few good action photos over the years. This roving pass allowed me to move around the Richfield Coliseum and to have access to the locker rooms and other areas. Basically I was able to roam wherever I wanted to before, during and after the fight. I got to see who was in the crowd, watch their reactions and see the fight from different angles.

There is no reason for me to write a recap round by round of this fight. Muhammad Ali was not at his best for this defense, in fact looked a bit out of shape to me. Chuck Wepner? Well, Chuck was just Chuck. Never a great fighter on his best days, what he was however was game. He was a brawler, a guy who wasn't afraid to take a punch in order to land a punch in return. His face was a road map of scars from previous battles. I had seen him get chopped up in three rounds against Joe Bugner in 1970 while in London.

It has been written many times that the Ali-Wepner fight was the inspiration for Sylvester Stallone's "Rocky". Thinking about it later on, it was easy to see how Sly Stallone grasped this fight as the idea for his Rocky series.

Going into this fight I was one of many who didn't give Wepner the slightest chance at winning or even coming close to it. He was a 40-1 underdog on most betting. At best Wepner was considered a fringe contender. He met a lot of top fighters of the day and actually was on an eight bout winning streak heading into the Ali match. His best wins during the streak came against Terry Hinke, Ernie Terrell and Randy Neumann twice. During his career to this point he had already lost nine fights. His losses were to Bob Stallings, Buster Mathis, Jerry Tomasetti, Jose Roman, George Foreman, Sonny Liston, Joe Bugner, Jerry Judge and Randy Neumann. He met a lot of the best but wasn't good enough to get over the hump to greatness. He was so prone to cuts that he was called "The Bayonne Bleeder" and thus many of his losses were stoppages because of cuts.

The biggest surprise of the fight came in the 9th round when Wepner threw a right hand to Ali's body and down he went. Referee Tony Perez, perhaps my least favorite referee of all time, immediately ruled it a knockdown and picked up the count. All during the fight Perez allowed Wepner to get away with rabbit punches. I could go on and on about other fights where I felt he did a terrible job. This time however, at least in ruling it a knockdown I will cut him some slack. On face value it looked to be legit. It turned out to be a tainted knockdown. What really happened was as Wepner launched his right hand he stepped on Ali's right foot and as the punch landed and Ali's foot was released, he sort of catapulted backwards in a slingshot reaction and fell. A beautiful photograph by Marvin Greene of the Plain Dealer in Cleveland actually captured the moment when Wepner stepped on Ali's foot.

That being said the heroic Wepner continued to wage war on Ali but took lots of punishment in return. Finally late in the 15th round with only seconds to go, Ali landed a series of punches and a final right that sent Chuck into the ropes and down. He arose at eight but was helpless and the fight was stopped.

The fight was disappointing in many ways, disappointing because Ali appeared out of shape and off his game. Although I wasn't the biggest Ali fan I admired his ability and felt he might have taken Wepner lightly. Also Ali's brother shouted several racial slurs from the corner a couple times during the bout. That was ugly. The crowd was papered with friends and celebrities from entertainment, sports and politics. The great Joe Louis was there, famous football coach Hank Stram, comedian Red Foxx, singer Lloyd Price, of course Joe Frazier and others too numerous to mention. The roving pass allowed me to mix among these greats. That was an amazing time for me. I will always be grateful to Jeff Temkin, who handled the press for the fight and issued me the Roving Photographers Pass. Many will remember Jeff as the ring announcer in a couple of the Rocky movies and The Champ remake in 1979. A good guy who sadly died in a car accident in California in 1982, at the very young age of 35.

It was a Muhammad Ali fight.....that is why it is one of my favorites.

22

PALM SPRINGS, CALIFORNIA
OCTOBER 15, 1977

I have always given credit to being in the right place at the right time for my being able to experience some amazing things in boxing. I fully realize that some of my experiences in boxing for over fifty years weren't preordained or planned. When I was able to attend certain fight cards sometimes it was just dumb luck, fate if you want to call it that. Although many of my favorite fights weren't classic in the truest sense, they have remained in my mind as favorites over the years because of the special circumstances or events that happened during those shows.

During one of my many California trips during the years 1975-85, I went to a fight show in Palm Springs, California. My wonderful friend George Luckman and a more recent friend, Dick Mastro and I drove down to the desert in October of 1977 to witness a fight card being put on by Mickey "The Kid" Davies. As always I looked forward to going for many reasons, one being I had never been to Palm Springs and I always loved traveling and experiencing new places.

Dick Mastro was the brother of Earl Mastro an excellent featherweight out of Chicago, who once fought for the NBA World Championship, losing a majority decision to Bat Battalino, on November 4, 1931. Dick was also a former fighter and over the years had been an actor and promoter in California. By the time we became friends Dick was putting out the Official Boxing Record, which was a neat little publication that kept track of upcoming fights and boxer's records. It was always rewarding spending time with him. He was just one of many people that I was introduced to by George Luckman.

The fight card was held at the California Angels minor league ballpark, "Angels Stadium". My reasoning for listing this fight, rather series of fights among my favorites has nothing to necessarily do with the fight action held that night. The card featured Mike Koranicki drawing in ten rounds with Samoan, Fili Moala, Jimmy Heair stopping Juan Garcia in the tenth round and Bakersfield favorite, Ruben Castillo winning a ten round decision over Miguel Meza.

The memories of this evening are many. First of all many celebrities attended and I was fortunate to meet and talk with several of them. Fighters such as Ken Norton and Bossman Jones were there. Frankie Crawford, former Clevelander who made a name for himself as an excellent featherweight was there too. Frankie had been paralyzed by a gun shot and was in a wheelchair. We spoke briefly about Cleveland and his career, but it was a sad conversation and not long after that evening Frankie took his own life.

I bumped into Eddie Futch in the men's room, and we talked about a lot of things on the way out. I recall him telling me he was going back to Philadelphia to try and talk Joe Frazier out of fighting again. I got the impression Joe felt he could still fight and was working hard to land some matches. Apparently Eddie Futch's advice to Joe was taken to heart because except for his fight with Jumbo Cummings in 1981 he did quit boxing. Eddie Futch by the way was not only an excellent trainer but a class act all the way.

Also in attendance was former fighter Martin Burke, who fought many excellent light-heavy and heavyweight fighters in his career from 1919-1929, including Gene Tunney and Cleveland's Johnny Risko. With him was his son, Hollywood actor, Paul Burke, perhaps most famous for being on the WWII television drama, "Twelve O' Clock High".

Perhaps my biggest memory of the Palm Springs evening however was something completely different. Just before the main event it appeared a cloud had closed in on the ring. It turned out to be a swarm of grasshoppers like something out of the Bible or a Hollywood epic. Maintenance crews came into the ring with brooms and swept the insects away, but they kept coming. Eventually order was restored but needless to say it was still a mess. A few of the grasshoppers lingered and were stepped on by the fighters.

Hollywood royalty had houses in Palm Springs, including Frank Sinatra and Bob Hope. On that evening we viewed Bob Hope's house up on the hill, with charring on the roof from a recent fire. Although October, it was plenty hot and very dry and we were happy to get into the air-conditioning of our car on the drive back to LA. As I wrote down my notes, my fight report for a now forgotten boxing magazine, I just couldn't help but think what an unusual yet special night this had been for me.

23

SUGAR RAY LEONARD-ROBERTO DURAN I
JUNE 20, 1980 (MONTREAL, CANADA)

When Sugar Ray Leonard and Roberto Duran met for the first time in Montreal I was not able to see it live. But my good friend Jim Jacobs sold me a 16mm copy of the fight and it arrived just a few days after the event.

Obviously I knew the results of the battle when the film arrived but not having seen it I was really excited to be able to view it so quickly. I did enjoy the fact that most of my close boxing friends had not seen it either. So I quickly put it on my projector, popped open the screen and sat back for the enjoyment. I was not disappointed that is for sure. It was a thrilling fight.

A few days later I entertained a large group of people at a local pub to raise funds for our new gym in Parma, Ohio. I had permission from Jim Jacobs so it was a win-win for me. It turned out to be an exciting night. It was one of those things where even though everyone knew the results of the fight, seeing it was still very special. This is the same gym that Roberto Duran finished up his training in 1981, for his first comeback fight against Nino Gonzalez, after his infamous "No Mas" fight with Sugar Ray Leonard.

I loved Roberto Duran as a lightweight, although I have to admit I liked Ken Buchanan a lot and did not like the way their title fight ended. I felt Ken was fouled. In time I came to really appreciate Duran's skills as a fighter. Till this day I rate him really high as a lightweight, historically.

This Roberto Duran-Sugar Ray Leonard fight was more than entertaining, it had a certain buzz about it. Sugar Ray, after winning the Olympics as a Lt-welter in 1976, rolled through his opponents before grasping the welterweight title from Wilfred Benitez on November 30, 1979, via a 15-rd TKO, in Las Vegas. By the time Leonard and Duran were signed to meet for the first time Leonard was undefeated and had defended his title once against Dave "Boy" Green in March of 1980, winning by a knockout in the 4th round.

Roberto Duran had only lost one fight in his seventy-three fight career leading up to the Sugar Ray Leonard fight. After winning the lightweight championship against Ken Buchanan in 1972, Duran had defended it twelve times. Moving up in weight was not a given but Duran's greatness was.

The fight itself lived up to expectations. There was a lot of give and take and gamesmanship. At the end Duran won the decision. I have always felt the main reason Sugar Ray Leonard lost is that he didn't fight the smartest fight of his career. He seemed to think he had to show his "macho" side

My Favorite Fights

and stood toe to toe with Duran at times, rather than boxing more.

The fight showed early on that Sugar Ray Leonard had no real plan to box Duran. As early as the second round he was staggered by a left hook. He proved he could take it but it probably was not the smartest strategy for him to use.

In rounds eleven and thirteen it was a battle of give and take where one fighter appeared to be in control only to have the other come back and take the play away. The action for the most part was furious and Duran appeared to be a man possessed.

The fight was an all action fight for the most part but I personally did not like the way referee Carlos Padilla handled the fight. To me he broke the fighters way too much, never seemed to let them get in close. It is one thing to let fighters hang on and slow the fight and make it boring, but it is another to stop a fighter when he is inside and possibly about to do damage.

All in all it was a super exciting fight. In the end the original announcement had two judges voting for Duran and one calling it a draw. It turned out that the third card had not been added correctly and the final tally had Roberto Duran winning a unanimous decision in taking Sugar Ray's title from him.

The Author with Roberto Duran (above) and (below) with Carmen Basilio (author's collection)

24

SUGAR RAY ROBINSON-CARMEN BASILIO I
SEPTEMBER 23, 1957 (NEW YORK)

Most boxing experts consider Sugar Ray Robinson the best fighter pound for pound ever. It is hard to argue that point when looking at his accomplishments. Personally I have always felt that when he was a welterweight he was the best ever. His only loss during those years was an over-the-weight fight with Jake LaMotta in 1943. This was Robinson's only loss to LaMotta in their six fight series. When Sugar Ray eventually won the middleweight title from LaMotta in 1951, his record stood at 120-1-2 with 78 knockouts.

Robinson had won the welterweight championship on December 20, 1946 with a 15-round decision over Tommy Bell for the vacant title. He then defended that title four times. One of his title defenses was his ill-fated match with Jimmy Doyle in Cleveland on June 24, 1947. Sugar Ray had a dream the night before that he killed Doyle and he tried to get the fight postponed. It didn't happen. He knocked out Doyle in the 8th round and sadly Doyle died the next day after surgery. Robinson then had three other successful title defenses against Chuck Taylor, Bernard Docusen and Kid Gavilan before deciding to campaign in the middleweight division.

Carmen Basilio will always hold a special place in my heart and memory. The first live fight I ever saw was in February of 1957 when, at the age of only ten, I witnessed Basilio stop former champion Johnny Saxton in two rounds at the Cleveland Arena. This was in defense of his welterweight crown. It was a total surprise that I would even be at a fight at such a young age but it happened. It will always be special for me even if the fight itself was not all that remarkable.

Carmen Basilio and I eventually met for the first time in 1978 and our paths crossed many times over the years, mostly in Rochester, New York. It was always special to see Carmen and I felt a bit of a kinship with him and enjoyed kidding around with him. I loved listening to his stories, especially when former opponents like Tony DeMarco or Gene Fullmer were in attendance. Upstate New Yorkers considered him a hero and for good reason.

Carmen Basilio to me could have been put on a poster and the title would have been "Courage" or even "Warrior". When I think of his career and his many battles I picture a battered face and a man driven to succeed. Never say die was his attitude and anyone who entered the ring with him knew they would be in a battle for sure. He was a man of courage and determination. Carmen met all of the best fighters in the welterweight division. That list is like a who's who of the division; Vic Cardell, Chuck Davey, Billy Graham, Ike Williams, Pierre Langlois, Tony DeMarco, Gil Turner, and Johnny Saxton.

Sugar Ray Robinson won the middleweight title from Jake LaMotta in February of 1951, lost it to England's Randy Turpin in July of 1951, won it back from Turpin in September of 1951, then defended it twice in 1952 against Bobo Olson and Rocky Graziano. Then he attempted to become a champion in three divisions as he took on Cleveland's Joey Maxim in June of 1952 for the light-heavyweight crown. The heat did him in at Yankee Stadium and he couldn't answer the bell for the 14th round. He had a big lead at the time but as Joey Maxim often said, "Hey I was fighting in that heat too."

Robinson retired after the Maxim fight. Bobo Olson and Randy Turpin were matched for the vacant title in October of 1953 with Olson coming out on top after 15-rounds. Bobo defended his newly won title three times, even tried to win the light-heavyweight title from Archie Moore during his reign as middleweight champ. He was unsuccessful in that bid. Then he decided to give a come-backing Sugar Ray Robinson a shot at his middleweight crown. Bobo Olson was a good fighter but he never could defeat Sugar Ray Robinson and was promptly relieved of his crown in two rounds on December 9, 1955.

Robinson gave Olson one more chance to win back the middleweight championship in May of 1956, but Olson only lasted two more rounds than the previous fight. In January of 1957 Robinson's rollercoaster ride as middleweight champion once again took a turn as Gene Fullmer won the title from him with a 15-round decision in New York.

Sugar Ray Robinson would win the middleweight title for the fourth time in a return match in May of 1957 with perhaps the most picture perfect left hook you could ever hope to see as he stopped Fullmer in the 5th round. It would be the only time in his long career that Gene Fullmer ever was counted out.

Which brings us to the first Robinson-Basilio fight on September 23, 1957 in Yankee Stadium. Sugar Ray Robinson had one of the best records in boxing history. While Carmen Basilio couldn't compete with his stats he did have a very respectable record of 51-12-7 with 24 knockouts heading into the fight with Sugar Ray. Considering the caliber of fighters he met, it was nothing to sneeze at. Robinson had an almost unbelievable record of 140-5-2.

The fight itself was a good one, to some degree even great. Robinson had the better record, had a seven pound weight advantage, was taller and had a longer reach. The one thing that he didn't have however was a bigger heart than Carmen. Nobody did.

38,072 fans watched the contest in Yankee Stadium in New York City. For the first ten rounds it was a pretty even fight. Sugar Ray would start out each round the way he usually did with his excellent left jab shooting out as Carmen ducked in low bobbing and weaving and trying to land his left hook. Somewhere during the third and fourth rounds Carmen was cut over his left eye. It continued to bleed throughout the fight but was never a factor.

Basilio was consistent in that he forced the fight throughout. Sometimes he would get in good shots, other times he took some leather but he never stopped coming. Robinson was throwing left hooks and straight rights but they didn't seem to discourage Carmen.

In the 11th round things really got interesting with some of the best exchanges of the fight. Near the end of the round Basilio caught Robinson on the ropes and punished him with both hands. With about 30 seconds left in the round Robinson took over and returned some heavy shots of his own.

In the 12th round Sugar Ray landed some excellent left hooks, then some overhand rights as he rallied and appeared to be taking over. But he also expended a lot of energy and the fact he was six years older than Carmen seemed to be catching up with him. It was still anyone's fight at this stage as neither man had really taken charge to assure victory.

In the 13th round Robinson did appear to tire. The two men had not clinched a lot during most of the contest but Robinson several times grabbed Basilio during this round to catch his breath. At the end of the round Robinson did however launch one of his late rallies with 30 seconds to go.

In the 14th round even Carmen showed he was a bit weary himself as Robinson jabbed and tried to pile up points. Yet Carmen continued to fight back, to press the fight, to keep his arms moving and did not let Sugar Ray get set to launch big countering punches.

The final round saw both men touch gloves and the crowd cheered loudly. Robinson's mouth was open but he continued to jab and did land a good right hand near the end of the round. Still in was not a fight where anyone watching knew for sure who had won until the scorecards were read. When the final bell sounded the crowd roared its approval. Everyone waited for the results and ring announcer Johnny Addie read off the scores. Judge Artie Aidala called it 9-5-1 for Basilio, referee Al Burl saw it 9-6 Robinson and the deciding vote by judge Bill Recht saw Basilio winning 8-6-1. Carmen was the new World Middleweight Champion!

The fight was truly exciting and called by Ring Magazine "The Fight of the Year". This would be the second of four consecutive years that Carmen Basilio was involved in that award. For his effort Basilio received $211,679 of the gate, while Robinson got $566,467.

Carmen Basilio will always be one of my favorite fighters of all time. It is only fitting that he was involved in more than one of my favorite fights.

A personalized, signed photo from the great Sugar Ray (author's collection).

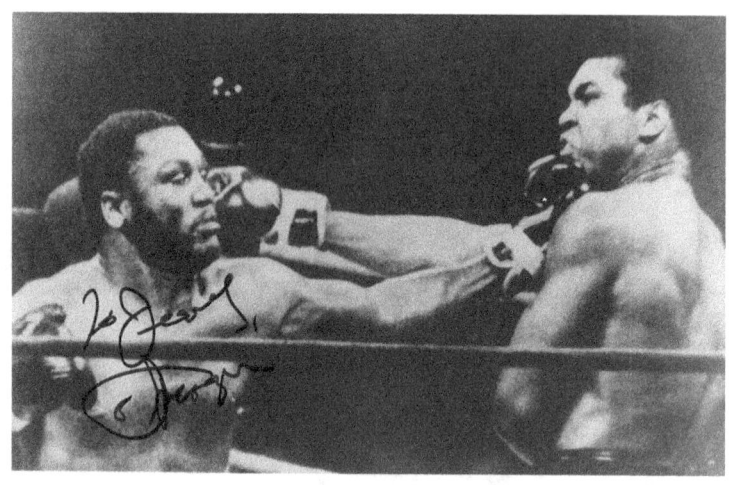

Frazier lands a left on Ali (author's collection).

25

MUHAMMAD ALI-JOE FRAZIER I

MARCH 8, 1971 (NEW YORK CITY)

Historians will always debate which of the great fights were indeed the greatest of all time. I suppose depending on which era these historians lived in would determine which fight they considered the best. During my time following boxing, starting in the late 50s and continuing up until the late 80s, early 90s, when I started to lose interest in boxing, I cannot think of a fight that affected me more than the first Ali-Frazier fight in 1971. One can debate that there have been greater fights but, in my mind, I have not experienced a fight that seemed more significant than this one which has forever been called, "The Fight of the Century".

As I have admitted before I was a Joe Frazier fan. I loved his style, I love his history, I loved the fact he fought his way up the ranks of contenders with a blue collar style and a rip-roaring attack. His hard work and constant pressure in the ring was something I certainly could not relate to. Don't get me wrong, I was a rank amateur with limited experience but my style was just the opposite of Smokin' Joe. I used a left jab and movement. Nobody would ever accuse me of seeking to slug it out with my opponents. I was not some brave brawler, I liked to hit and not be hit as much as I could.

One would think I would be more of a Muhammad Ali fan than Joe Frazier fan based on the fact I tried to be a boxer and not a slugger. Muhammad Ali in his early days was a master boxer who basically rarely got hit. Until his refusal to be inducted into the United States Army and the eventual stripping of his license, I didn't see any way he would be defeated.

I did have personal conflicts about Ali in my own mind. First of all I felt the two Liston fights were fishy in many ways. One can argue Liston simply quit in the first fight, knew he wasn't going to win. Still I could never rap my mind around how a big bad fearless fighter like Liston lost his title sitting on the stool. Watching the film and seeing him throwing jabs it didn't look like he had any shoulder injury as he later claimed. The rematch stunk to the high heavens and nobody will ever convince me that Liston didn't take a dive in that one. Was it a fix? Was Ali even part of it or aware of it, did Liston just decide to take the money and run, was he threatened? Nobody will ever know for sure, especially since most all of the principles involved are gone now. If anyone wants to believe that the right Ali threw was a legit knockout punch, that is their opinion and I am not going to debate it.

The second thing that caused a conflict in my thought process was the fact I was drafted into the Army in February of 1966 as were many of my friends and relatives. I am not a political person most of the time but I felt Ali's sudden reasons for not stepping forward were rather timely on his part. Whether he was totally sincere is not for me to say. I think I can safely say he was not going anywhere near the combat zone in Viet Nam if he had answered the call. He would have been entertaining troops, you could take that to the bank. His choice was his choice and he paid the price for his convictions as far as his overall career goes.

By the time Ali and Frazier were set to fight I had long since gotten over the draft thing. I got out in 1968 and have never regretted serving my country, in fact I am quite proud of it. I was able to spend a few private moments with Muhammad over the years, once just the two of us in a hotel room. It is not my place to sit in judgment about his personal life, what he did or didn't do. My focus has been on his fighting ability and his fights. Only a fool would say that he was not one of the best heavyweights ever and did a lot of wonderful things in his life. Love him or hate him, you have to give him credit for that. To say during his lifetime he was one of the most recognized people in the world would be factual.

Leading up to this fight it was exciting, it was electrifying. After all, you had two undefeated fighters with two different followings. The pro-Frazier fans probably disliked Ali a lot, especially the way he talked about Joe, the name calling and the outward disrespect. The Ali fans of course felt that he had been robbed of some of his prime years. They are probably correct. They felt because Muhammad had never lost the title in the ring, he was the rightful champion. Still to me Muhammad Ali, even after losing some of his best years, was better than anyone else in the ring and many felt better than Frazier too.

I can't truthfully say I felt Joe Frazier was going to win the match against Ali. I was rooting for him, but I never would have placed a bet or was confident enough to think he would pull it off for sure.

The Ali-Frazier fight was a happening, a huge event. Not only did Madison Square Garden sell out quickly, but it also attracted a huge amount of celebrities from stage, screen, music and fashion. The people who attended the fight were for the most part dressed to the nines as they say. Singer Diana Ross of The Supremes was there, actors Dustin Hoffman and Burt Lancaster. Jack Dempsey, Gene Tunney and other famous fighters and celebrities adorned the arena. Frank Sinatra was hired by Life Magazine to be one of their photographers at ringside. Frank did a good enough job that several of his photos were used including the cover photo for the March 16, 1971 edition of Life Magazine. Burt Lancaster did color commentary with Don Dunphy.

In my *50 Years of Fights, Fighters and Friendships* I mentioned that I was a nervous wreck watching the fight at a close-circuit showing at the Yorktown Theater in Cleveland. My knees were knocking and I was on the edge of my seat the entire fight. I watched every moment but I have to admit I had no clue who officially might be winning the fight, although Frazier seemed ahead. The knockdown in the 15th round told me that Ali had lost for sure. Judge Artie Aidala voted 9-6 for Frazier, judge Bill Recht voted a rather lopsided 11-4 for Frazier and referee, Arthur Mercante called it 8-6-1 even.

Over the years I have viewed this fight many times, first on film, then video and finally on DVD. Seeing it in a calm manner, knowing the results, not having any reason to be nervous I realized that Ali was mostly flat-footed during the fight. In a couple of rounds he tried to get up on his toes, but he didn't have that old bounce. I also realized that he clowned way too much.

Arthur Mercante would later say he felt Ali gave away a few rounds. I will agree and Mercante had to constantly warn Ali to stop holding behind the neck. This is not to say Muhammad didn't fight his heart out. Joe's face was a lumpy mess by the end of the fight as Ali landed many left-right combinations. He also missed many punches and in some rounds he didn't do much, he laid on the ropes and mocked Joe. Both fighters were warned several times about talking by Mercante.

Joe Frazier was in excellent shape and kept coming the whole fight. He weighed 205 1/2 while Ali weighed 215. Ali looked in shape physically too but in hindsight there is no doubt in my mind he lost something during the three years in exile. When he took a round off, Frazier just continued trying to launch his vaulted left hooks. Joe worked to the body, that was his fight plan and he stuck to it.

In round eleven, near the end of the round, Frazier landed a big punch that staggered Ali and he stumbled back into the ropes. Although he clowned and wobbled and acted like he was hurt to try and psych out Frazier, there is no doubt in my mind Ali was seriously hurt. His legs were failing him.

The knockdown in the 15th round was legit. What impressed me most was how quickly Ali got up. He took the eight count. Not many would have gotten up from that shot.

No matter how you viewed this fight, no matter who was your favorite, how you scored it then or now, to me it ranks as one of the most exciting fights ever. It had all of the elements in it, all the drama. There may never be an encounter like this again because the circumstances were just perfect for this to be known as "The Fight of The Century".

ACKNOWLEDGMENTS

First of all I have to acknowledge that my late father, Ralph "Bud" Fitch was the first person to ever expose me to boxing. Not a big fan of the sport he did, however, occasionally watch boxing on our first television in the 1950s. Because of that I too saw glimpses of those fights. My dad was always good to me but I seriously doubt he had any inkling back then that boxing would be such a big part of my life for so many years.

The late, great Jim Jacobs was a generous man who also happened to have the world's largest collection of fight films. Jim sold me several copies of my favorite fights including some that involved Cleveland fighters. I will always be grateful for his kindness.

What can I say about Jim Amato? The former Clevelander has a rich love for Cleveland sports and boxing in general. He has written countless stories for numerous publications and websites over the years. Recently he has written his first book "Gloves Gone By". I consider him a special friend and appreciate his kindness in writing the Foreword for this book.

Harry Otty is a man who I have been indebted to for many years. He has been the main man in putting together my last four books. A talented writer himself, I can't imagine anyone I'd rather have do this chore.

As always I want to thank my son Tad. He is an amazing man and he has always been my biggest fan and my inspiration. Thank you Tad.

I am very thankful that the love of my life, Lynda, still agrees to edit my books, even though I know she'd rather be doing something else. Without her I would hate to think what my writing efforts would look like.

And a special thank you to all of you who have supported my writing efforts throughout the years.

ABOUT THE AUTHOR

Jerry Fitch was born in Cleveland, Ohio in 1946. Educated locally at Valley Forge High School, he started following boxing in the mid 1950s. Called by many one of America's leading boxing historians, he began writing in 1970 and since then has written hundreds of stories and essays for most of the world's leading boxing magazines including; The Ring, Boxing Illustrated, Boxing News (England), Boxing World (South Africa) and Boxing World (USA). He has traveled to many parts of the world and has met some of the greatest fighters of all time including; Jack Dempsey, Joe Louis, Rocky Marciano, Joe Frazier, Muhammad Ali, Tony Zale, Jimmy McLarnin, Billy Conn and Carmen Basilio to name a few.

This is Jerry's fifth book.

ALSO BY JERRY FITCH

Cleveland's Greatest Fighters of All Time

James Louis Bivins: The Man Who Would Be Champion

50 Years of Fights, Fighters and Friendships

Johnny Risko: The Cleveland Rubber Man

www.ingramcontent.com/pod-product-compliance
Lightning Source LLC
Chambersburg PA
CBHW071401290426
44108CB00014B/1639